Curling

STEPS TO SUCCESS

Sean M.R. Turriff

HUMAN KINETICS

Library of Congress Cataloging-in-Publication Data

Names: Turriff, Sean, 1969- author.
Title: Curling : steps to success / Sean Turriff.
Description: Champaign : Human Kinetics, [2016]
Identifiers: LCCN 2016012046 (print) | LCCN 2016031642 (ebook) | ISBN
  9781492515777 (print) | ISBN 9781492542650 (ebook)
Subjects: LCSH: Curling.
Classification: LCC GV845 .T87 2016 (print) | LCC GV845 (ebook) | DDC
  796.964--dc23
LC record available at https://lccn.loc.gov/2016012046

ISBN: 978-1-4925-1577-7 (print)

The web addresses cited in this text were current as of May 2016, unless otherwise noted.

Acquisitions Editor: Diana Vincer
Senior Developmental Editor: Cynthia McEntire
Managing Editor: Nicole Moore
Copyeditor: Patricia MacDonald
Senior Graphic Designer: Keri Evans
Cover Designer: Keith Blomberg
Photograph (cover): Photodisc/Getty Images
Photographs (interior): Anil Mungal
Visual Production Assistant: Joyce Brumfield
Photo Production Manager: Jason Allen
Art Manager: Kelly Hendren
Illustrations: © Human Kinetics
Printer: Premier Print Group

We thank the Richmond Hill Curling Club in Richmond Hill, Ontario, for assistance in providing the location for the photo shoot for this book.

Printed in the United States of America   10   9   8   7   6   5   4   3   2   1

Human Kinetics
Website: www.HumanKinetics.com

United States: Human Kinetics
P.O. Box 5076
Champaign, IL 61825-5076
800-747-4457
e-mail: info@hkusa.com

Canada: Human Kinetics
475 Devonshire Road Unit 100
Windsor, ON N8Y 2L5
800-465-7301 (in Canada only)
e-mail: info@hkcanada.com

Europe: Human Kinetics
107 Bradford Road
Stanningley
Leeds LS28 6AT, United Kingdom
+44 (0) 113 255 5665
e-mail: hk@hkeurope.com

Australia: Human Kinetics
57A Price Avenue
Lower Mitcham, South Australia 5062
08 8372 0999
e-mail: info@hkaustralia.com

New Zealand: Human Kinetics
P.O. Box 80
Mitcham Shopping Centre, South Australia 5062
0800 222 062
e-mail: info@hknewzealand.com

E6645

I dedicate this book to my wife Tracey Turriff. She is a ray of sunshine that lights up all those who know her with a glow from inside that seems to only ever grow brighter. She is a wonderful mother and wife, and I love her very much.

Contents

Climbing the Steps to Curling Success

To say that the sport of curling is unique is an understatement. Many aspects of the game are different from other sports, but even the perception of the game by people who don't play is unique. The majority of people, particularly in countries with colder winters, are at least familiar with the sport, and it is interesting that there is a significant fan base of people who will watch curling on television but who don't actually understand how the game is played let alone play themselves. Many fans who can be enticed to try the game fall in love with it for a variety of reasons, not the least of which is the broad range of skills and broad level of competition that the game offers. *Curling: Steps to Success* goes beyond an initial introduction of the sport of curling and gives players, coaches, and teachers of the game direction on all the fundamental aspects of the sport that must be mastered in order to be successful.

Many people are surprised to discover how accessible curling is. There is a misconception that the sport has some exclusivity associated with it, and a number of factors contribute to this. The reality is that the sport of curling is easy to pick up and easy to stay with for a lifetime. Once people get involved in the sport, they often find many reasons to keep themselves involved for the long term. The game can be played at a variety of levels across a broad age range. Men can play with women both competitively and socially. It's relatively inexpensive and requires a minimum of specialized equipment to get started. For the most part, the biggest hurdle people have to overcome when getting started is general inexperience with the sport, which creates some mystery around it. After all, there are no pickup curling games being played outside organized facilities.

The goal of *Curling: Steps to Success* is to introduce the sport to people unfamiliar with it and also to lay out a path for skill development for those who want to improve in the game. Understanding the basics of the game is relatively easy; however, players naturally want to develop their skills so that they see progression in their efforts. *Curling: Steps to Success* leads you through the fundamental skills the sport demands and helps you improve those skills. Regardless of your current level, *Curling: Steps to Success* will help you enjoy the game as you increase both your ability and confidence.

Curling: Steps to Success will also guide teachers and coaches who are interested in helping their athletes achieve more in the sport. The book identifies fundamental skills that athletes need to master and gives detailed instruction on technique and how to develop these skills. Drills and exercises as well as detailed descriptions of form will help instructors properly direct players toward success.

Curling: Steps to Success progresses through skills in a systematic way, continually building on previous fundamentals in order to provide a complete understanding of what is required to be a successful curler. For each step, follow this sequence:

1. Read the explanation of the skill covered in the step, why the step is important, and how to execute the step.
2. Study the photos and illustrations for a visual explanation of the step.
3. Read the instructions for the drills. Practice the drills and record your results.
4. Have a qualified observer evaluate your skill technique once you have completed each set of drills.
5. At the end of each step, review your performance and scores from the drills. Once you are satisfied with your performance level for that skill, move on to the next step.

Repetition is extremely important; however, following the steps precisely is the key to improving. Practice does not in fact make perfect. Practice makes permanent. Only perfect practice makes perfect permanently, so it is important that you repeat the skills with precision in order to master them. Approach each skill with patience, diligence, and an open mind. As you progress through the book, you will find areas that pose significant difficulties, but if you follow the steps as described, your skills will improve. Many of the drills have variations in difficulty. As you monitor your progress, push your skills further by using the drill variations.

Curling is a rich sport in that there are many rewards at many levels. It is a sport that people can participate in for life, and many do. Improving your skills will make the game more enjoyable, regardless of the level at which you play. *Curling: Steps to Success* will help you become the player you really want to be.

Acknowledgments

The path to success in any venture is a long and winding one with both challenges and rewards around every bend. Often that path is longer and more winding than people expect, and too often people give up just one turn away from the next success. What keeps you going down that road to discover new adventures and challenges? What is it that keeps you walking on a path that requires hard work with every single step? For me, it's the people in my life who are beside me, encouraging, supporting, and motivating me. The reward on this journey is not the destination but the people that I have with me through it all.

My family comes first in all things. I could write an entire book on what they mean to me and how they have supported me through my ongoing development as a coach. My wife, Tracey, and my boys, Jacob and Joshua, are my foundations. They give me balance in all things, and I would be nowhere without them beside me. Being as involved in the sport of curling as I am takes time and, specifically, time away from them, so their acceptance and encouragement not only keeps me going but pushes me to make that time worthwhile. Any time I can't be with them better be time well spent, otherwise I'm shortchanging them. They are my biggest fans and never cease to amaze me with their enthusiasm towards this sport. I love them all and could never thank them enough for helping me be who I am.

Outside of my family, I have been blessed to have met a large number of people who have become mentors, inspirations, and friends on my journey as a curling coach. From outside the sport, curling coaches must seem like an odd bunch. It is a close and welcoming fraternity of people who are quick to help each other and who see the growth of their colleagues not as competition, but as growth for the sport as a whole. We talk together as colleagues and work together as friends.

My coaching journey began out of my own love for the game, and while I had a passion within myself, very early on the fire was stoked by someone I'm now proud to call my colleague, Jennifer Ferris. She was one of my first coaching instructors and opened doors for me not only in terms of introducing opportunities to me, but also in terms of how to think like a coach. I would not be a coach at all if it weren't for Jen and her infectious enthusiasm for curling and coaching.

Infectious is also a good term for my good friend and coaching colleague Maurice Wilson. Maurice and I met at a curling camp where he mentored a team I was coaching and somehow we hit it off. Over the years as our friendship grew, I've strived to achieve his level of knowledge and to adapt his easygoing yet serious approach to the art of coaching. Somehow Maurice makes this look easy, and I admire that greatly.

I knew of Bill Tschirhart long before I ever had the pleasure of meeting him. When I was just starting out as a coach, I received some life altering advice from him at a time when he had no idea who I was. That advice clarified the road ahead more than Bill will likely ever realize. He was generous and encouraging to this stranger and from that moment on I became a lifelong fan of his. In the years since, I've been fortunate enough to get to know Bill a little better and consider him the benchmark for coaching. His example is another that I will spend my life striving towards.

I am also extremely fortunate that someone, somewhere once had a conversation with Jim Waite where my name was mentioned. I cannot thank that unknown someone enough because it resulted in Jim giving me a chance to work with him and some of the best coaches and people in Canada at the Trillium Curling Camp held every summer in Ontario, Canada. While I've had many milestones in my coaching career, the opportunities that he has given me and the support he's extended to me really changed my life. I can say for certain that I would not have written this book if it were not for Jim Waite. I can also say for certain that I would be a small fraction of the coach I am today if it were not for his support. Jim does that for people, and I consider myself extremely fortunate to have fallen under his influence.

I would also like to thank the Richmond Hill Curling Club. The photos in this book were taken there, and the support the club executive and manager, John Majnarich, have given me has been wonderful. The models you see in those photos also deserve recognition. These are friends of mine who gave up their time to be part of this. To Pedro Malvar, Cassie Paccanaro, Tyler Stewart, Sarah Chettiar, Kateryna Tepylo, and Nicole Westlund Stewart, thank you so very much for being so photogenic.

I also need to thank the team at Human Kinetics who helped me through this book writing journey. I've been amazed at the support and insight that I've received along the way. The whole team there has been incredible all the way through this. I want to specifically thank Cynthia McEntire, Nicole Moore, and Diana Vincer. These three have kept me on track and have miraculously made sense of the things I put to page, and I'm truly grateful.

Finally, I want to thank all the athletes that I've had the pleasure of coaching over the years. I can't name you all because there are just too many of you, but I can say I've learned something from each and every one of you. You have all contributed to my own development and have made my coaching journey exciting and rewarding beyond all expectations.

I hope you enjoy the book, and I hope it makes you a better curler and person.

The Sport of Curling

It will probably never be definitively known why in the mid-16th century someone decided to challenge a rival by sliding a stone along the surface of a frozen pond in Scotland. Nor will it likely be understood just how this activity gained popularity to the point where clubs formed in the 19th century, specifically around sliding stones down sheets of ice. It is clear, however, that the game did originate on those frozen lochs and ponds in Scotland and that it was exported by the Scots to what ever icy locales they may have settled. The strange and wonderful challenge of pushing rocks along frozen rivers gained more and more traction over the years and eventually became a full blown sport. The first recorded rules for a curling game were eventually drawn up in 1838 in Edinburgh at the Grand Caledonia Curling Club, which still serves as the central location for Scottish curling and is not far from where those first stones were thrown.

From convenient natural ice settings, the game has evolved to an indoor sport that is played practically the world over. No longer limited to the cold winter countries where the game originally gained popularity, curling has migrated to many places where other winter sports aren't popular or convenient. Curling has taken unlikely root in countries such as Turkey, Spain, Brazil, Israel, Australia, New Zealand, Qatar, and even the U.S. Virgin Islands; as you will see, while it can be difficult to make ice in many of these places, this explosion in popularity is not that difficult to understand. This growth has been accelerated even further by the introduction of the discipline of mixed doubles.

In many ways, the sport of curling suffers from an identity crisis. In 1998 it was introduced at the Nagano Winter Olympic Games as a full medal sport, bringing a level of legitimacy and professionalism that had not been as widely recognized up until then. Curling had been a part of the Olympics on and off since the 1924 Games in Chamonix, France, where a men's competition was held. Its inclusion as a full medal event is responsible for introducing a much wider audience to the sport and has significantly increased interest in the game worldwide. Many countries that had previously never had any curling background or experience have since introduced national curling programs with the hopes of sending teams to the Olympics. Today, the sport is one of the most viewed events of the Winter Games, particularly on television. The success of the standard version and a positive response to the sport in general has led to the addition of mixed doubles curling at the 2018 Olympics.

Before its Olympic success, however, the sport was seen very differently, and although the popularity of curling has flourished, much of that previous impression remains. Curling has a rich history and has built up significant tradition around both game play and events in general. This history has been a very attractive part of what brings new players to the game and more importantly what keeps people involved with the sport. Typically, new curlers are introduced to the game through an existing personal connection. Often family members bring new players into curling clubs, and these existing social connections among participants create an intimate atmosphere around the game. Events at the local level reflect this feeling of inclusion and are usually very social affairs. In fact, even players at the highest levels still highly value the personal connection among all competitors and will cite it as a major reason for their continued participation in the sport. A social aspect this significant across all levels of the game is rare for any sport, let alone an Olympic one.

The perception of curling as a social activity is an attraction, yet it is also a barrier that the sport has needed to overcome in order to gain some measure of legitimacy in the sporting world. For many, curling looked like only a social activity with no true sporting component. Many people still do not fully understand the physical demands and skills that are required in order to qualify the sport as an Olympic event and to play it at the highest levels. Rather, they see the social nature of play at the initial levels and assume the game does not progress much past that.

Curling is growing in popularity in large part because of its inclusion in the Olympic Winter Games; however, that is simply a vehicle for introducing the sport to the masses. The real following comes from those who are inspired to try the game and who fall in love with it.

CURLING FACILITIES

Curling is played in many types of facilities around the world, and aside from the high-profile, highest-level competitions, the nature of these facilities often reflects the maturity of the sport in each country. Canada has the greatest number of curlers as a country and boasts nearly 1,200 dedicated curling facilities. Many other countries share ice facilities with other sports, such as hockey, to take advantage of existing facility equipment. Dedicated facilities are ideal for creating and maintaining good playing conditions; however, they cannot always be economically justified, forcing the use of the shared facility model. Dedicated facilities can have any number of sheets of ice to play on, and the number of sheets within a facility often depends on factors such as the proximity to other facilities and the size of the local population. At higher levels of competition, curling is played in large arenas to accommodate fans. Dedicated facilities typically will have a lounge at one end of the playing area where games can be watched; however, the lounge areas will only accommodate a small number of viewers. The lounges are intended as both a viewing area and as an area for players to socialize after games. For larger competitions, bigger venues are needed.

Facilities often provide basic equipment such as brushes and sliders so that people new to the game do not have to invest in expensive equipment in order to get started. Rocks are always part of the facility equipment and as we will see in subsequent chapters, they are handled with great care by facility management.

ICE

Although it is commonly known that curling is played on ice, less commonly understood is the specific nature of curling ice and how it differs from other sporting ice surfaces such as those used in hockey. If there is an analogy to be made, curling ice is much more like a golf green than a golf fairway in terms of the effort made to create and maintain it. In many ways, it is a minor miracle that curling physically works with the precision that it does. Stones traveling down a sheet of curling ice can be affected by a large number of factors, and great care is taken to ensure modern ice surfaces are as consistent as possible.

This level of care starts with the type of water used to create curling ice. First, the water is much more pure than that used in other ice sports in order to minimize contaminants. Any contaminants in a sheet of ice will eventually migrate to the surface, where stones may slide over them. Material that gets under a stone will randomly affect its path and ruin shots.

Curling ice is also much more level than other sporting ice surfaces. Curling rocks will be affected by a level change as little as 0.05 millimeter over the width of a sheet. Significant low spots or high spots on a curling sheet will negatively affect game play by making areas of the sheet difficult to play on. Maintaining this precision of level is made even more difficult because of another requirement for curling ice: the pebble.

Most sporting ice surfaces are created to be smooth on the usable surface, but not curling ice. A considerable amount of science is involved in what makes ice slippery. Suffice it to say, smooth ice is actually much stickier than one might realize, and for this reason ice makers have to change the top surface of curling ice in order to make the game work. The ice maker walks down the sheet and applies a fine spray of hot water droplets to the playing surface. The mist rains down on the sheet and freezes, creating many randomly placed and randomly sized frozen bumps. These frozen bumps on the curling ice are aptly named the pebble (figure 1), and they reduce the

Figure 1 Pebble.

amount of friction between the curling stone and the ice surface. The size and the shape of these bumps have traditionally been black art within the curling world. In recent years, additional scientific study has been applied to this entire process, although precise application of pebble is still specific to the facility. In any case, without pebble, the effort to propel stones from one end of the sheet to the other would be far too great to allow for any precision, and there would be no curl to the path of the stones as they travel down the sheet. This curl is an essential part of the game.

The pebble is very sensitive to wear and tear. Naturally, it will wear unevenly during game play, both from stones running over the ice and from brushing. Because of this wear on the pebble, the precise paths the stones take down the sheet will be affected shot by shot. Since the pebble also determines how fast the stones travel, the force required to propel the stones down the sheet will change as the game progresses. Teams need to learn how to read these changes in ice conditions so they may accurately predict where stones will curl. Predicting shot outcomes is critical to the game. The ability to recognize changing ice conditions correctly and make the appropriate adjustments are natural parts of the game.

Heat has the biggest impact on the wear of the pebble. Pebble is nothing more than frozen drops of water on the ice surface and their height is very small, so it is very quickly and easily melted if care is not taken to protect it. Before their first use, stones are placed on a nonplaying area of the ice for at least 24 hours in order to cool them to the ice temperature. In dedicated facilities, stones are left on the ice surface for the majority of the season, removed only when ice maintenance is required. This is done so they do not warm up and transfer heat to the pebble during play, which would destroy the playing surface. However, rocks are not the only things that contact the ice during play. Players themselves come into contact with the ice in a number of ways and therefore must always take care not to apply heat to the playing surface. Body parts resting on the ice can leave impressions in as little as 3 seconds of contact, and these impressions cannot be fixed during a game. The shoes worn by players will also transfer heat to the playing surface if not properly cooled before game play. To prevent ice damage, all players should cool their shoes before taking any slides out of the hack. All that is required to accomplish this is to stand or slide on the ice for 30 seconds in a non-playing area of the sheet.

Keeping the ice clean during game play is another major consideration in curling. Stones traveling down the ice are very sensitive to any material that gets caught under them. Fibers are a typical hazard. Debris from equipment such as brush heads or worn shoes can also damage the playing surface and affect stones in play. Both maintenance staff and players take great care to keep the ice surface as clean as possible.

Before each game, a fresh application of pebble is applied (figure 2), and then it is common to use a nipper to cut off the top of the ice pebble before game play (figure 3). A nipper is nothing more than an unheated blade with a handle that can be pushed down the sheet of ice. The frozen pebble is naturally uneven, and if game play starts on the uncut pebble, the ice will be more difficult to play on until the tops of that pebble start to level out.

Some facilities drag a set of rocks up and down the sheet to break the tops off the pebble. This is a much less desirable way to level off the pebble because it damages the structure of the pebble by cracking it, causing it to break down

Figure 2   Icemaker creating pebble.

Figure 3   Icemaker nipping the ice.

much faster during the game and therefore negatively affecting play. Icemakers go through a considerable amount of effort to create the ideal size, shape, and amount of pebble so that it will last over the course of a curling game.

The amount of pebble will start to build up unevenly after multiple applications, so icemakers use specialized equipment with a heated blade to scrape the top surface off the ice (figure 4). To ensure level ice, it is essential that the scraper have a sharp, well-maintained blade with no nicks. Scraping is done regularly every two games or so. In dedicated facilities, more extensive ice maintenance is done multiple times a season. A deeper level of ice is taken off to remove any impurities frozen into the surface and to ensure that the ice remains level across sheets.

Figure 4 Icemaker scraping curling ice.

CURLING SHEETS

The large pad of ice within a facility is divided into individual playing areas known as sheets. These divisions are usually marked by lines within the ice rather than with physical barriers, although the method for separating sheets can differ from facility to facility. A sheet of ice has definite markings and dimensions that are mostly common across all curling facilities (figure 5). Interestingly, although the size of the rings and the length of the sheet are exactly the same around the world, there is considerable variation in the width. This is mostly a result of how the rules evolved to encourage play across the breadth of the curling sheet and how that evolution manages to fit into existing facilities. Dedicated curling facilities are fixed and usually cannot accommodate a change in the width of the sheet. For this reason, rule books around the world typically identify a minimum and maximum sheet width. For example, the current World Curling Federation rule for the width of a curling sheet states that the width may be a minimum of 14 feet, 6 inches (4.4 m) and up to a maximum of 16 feet, 5 inches (5 m). That is a considerable difference but the tolerance is built in so that curling facilities don't need to do major renovations to accommodate rule changes.

A curling sheet looks like a long, skinny rectangle with sets of concentric rings at each end. The length of the sheet is and has been a fixed dimension for some time. The total length of a curling sheet is 150 feet (45.7 m), although the playing area is 126 feet (38.4 m) long. The remaining 24 feet (7.3 m) accommodates the hack and rock storage during play, with 12 feet (3.7 m) of ice behind the playing area at each end. The set of rings is commonly known as the house, and it is the scoring area. For points to be counted in a game, stones must come to rest at least partially covering a portion of

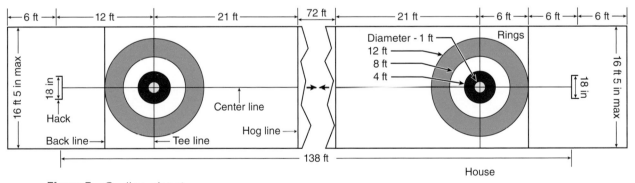

Figure 5 Curling sheet.

these rings when viewed from above the stone. A major skill in curling is the ability to accurately deliver a stone so that it stops in the rings, and so any variation between facilities in this regard would completely change the nature of the game.

It is important to understand the markings built into the sheet. Sheets usually border right on each other, and so the side lines mark where the playing area ends for a specific sheet. If a stone comes into contact with a side line, it is immediately removed from play because otherwise it would impose on a neighboring sheet. The back line identifies the length border for a specific sheet, and the outermost ring actually contacts this back line. Therefore, a portion of the back line is actually in the scoring area. For this reason, stones must completely cross the back line in order to be removed from play. This is completely different from how the bordering side line is used.

Behind the back line are the hacks (figure 6). Hacks look like starter blocks used by track athletes and are fixed into the ice by a variety of methods depending on the facility. The hacks serve the same purpose in curling as they do in track—to give athletes a place from which to push off. The hacks are generally made from rubber and are shaped to allow a comfortable foot placement in the delivery setup. There are two hacks at each end of the curling sheet, one for right-handed athletes and one for left-handed athletes. Hack location is specifically called out in the rules in the section on curling sheet dimensions.

A line runs down the center of the entire length of the sheet. Although this line is called out in rule books to help set the dimensions of the sheet, it has no rules associated with it. Its purpose is to help ice makers create and maintain the playing surface.

Bisecting the rings at a right angle to the center line is what is known as the tee line. This line has strategic importance in game play, but it also represents the point of no return for a delivery. Once a stone that is intended to be delivered has reached the tee line, it is considered in play and cannot be taken back. Before reaching this line, a player may abort the delivery and start the shot over again, though this is a rare occurrence.

Figure 6 Hacks.

The final line in the playing area is a thick line parallel to the tee line positioned 27 feet (8.2 m) from the back line. This line is oddly named the hog line for reasons often speculated on in folklore. The hog line marks the farthest distance a delivering player may hold onto the stone before releasing it. The penalty for a late release is that the stone delivered is pulled from play before another stone is delivered by the opposition. The hog lines also define the area in which stones may come to rest during game play.

Rocks delivered to the opposite end of the sheet may remain in play only if they have traveled past the far hog line and come to rest without touching a side line and without going past the back line. A rock that comes to rest before or in contact with the far hog line is immediately removed from play before any more stones are thrown. There are exceptions to this hog line rule, although they too are rarely seen in game play.

As previously mentioned, there are four concentric rings at each end of the sheet (figure 7). These rings are centered around a pin hole placed at the precise intersection of the tee line and center line. The outermost ring is 12 feet (3.7 m) in diameter, with 8-foot (2.4 m) and 4-foot (1.2 m) rings within it. These three rings are named for their diameter in feet. It is very common to hear reference to the "12 foot" for instance, which refers to the outermost ring. The size of the smallest ring, commonly known as the button, varies from facility to facility, although the rule book specifies a diameter of 1 foot (0.3 m). These rings are painted different colors, often based on club color schemes as much as anything else. Rocks are divided between teams based on handle color, and it is common for clubs to paint the rings to match the rock handles. There is no significance to matching the colors of stones to rings other than for style. It's common for the 12-foot ring to be painted either blue or red, with the 4-foot ring painted the remaining color. The 8-foot ring and the button are commonly left white. This creates four distinct rings on the playing surface. Some of this styling of rings is changing as technology allows for more complicated color schemes. It's becoming more common for curling rings to have advertising and other logos imprinted in them, but again this is purely for style and has no impact on game play.

Figure 7   Rings.

CURLING EQUIPMENT

Although curling requires a specific playing facility, the personal equipment is simple, which is a major attraction for people interested in trying the sport. As in any sport, as players become more competitive, the equipment options become more varied and tuned to players' specific performance needs. That being said, the basic equipment doesn't really change throughout the competitive slope.

Curling Stones

Every curling facility provides curling stones for game play. Curling stones are made from a very specific type of granite primarily mined from Ailsa Craig, a small island off the coast of Scotland. Other than a small vein found in Wales, the granite in Ailsa Craig is the only stone appropriate for making curling rocks.

Stones are ground to specific dimensions and weights per long-standing rules (figure 8). These dimensions factor into the sport considerably. Because of the long life of curling stones and the evolution of the game, the actual dimensions of the stones vary. Stones now must weigh between 38 and 44 pounds (17 to 20 kg) and must have a minimum height of 4.5 inches (11 cm) and a maximum circumference of 36 inches (91 cm). If it sounds odd for the essential playing piece of the game to have varying dimensions, it is. Again, this is a result of the limited resource from which the stones are made and the long life of a curling stone, which can be a hundred years or more with care. Stones are round and have a unique profile consisting of a flat striking band around their center, which allows them to very effectively transfer momentum when they contact each other during game play. The stones slide on a small flat ring ground on the bottom surface. Colored plastic handles affixed to the stones allow them to be delivered, and the color of the handles shows which team they belong to during game play.

Figure 8 Curling stone dimensions.

Curling Brushes

Each player requires a brushing device. Players can choose from a variety of curling brushes, all with slightly different advantages. The basic design consists of a shaft around 4 feet (1.2 m) long. At the bottom of the shaft is a cloth-covered foam head that contacts the ice. The size and shape of the brush head vary from manufacturer to manufacturer, as does the cloth material covering the foam. Considerable study has gone into the development of these materials to better understand the effect that brushing has on the ice surface. Ideally, the configuration of the brush and the material it is made from will help the brushers maximize the heat transfer to the pebble without destroying it. For instance, some abrasive cloth materials are highly effective at creating friction but ruin the running path after only a few shots.

Hair brushes are also commonly used. Instead of a cloth-covered foam piece (figure 9a), the hair brush (figure 9b) has a collection of hair sprouts made of hog hair or horse hair mounted on the brush head. This type of brush looks similar to a household cleaning brush.

Both types of brush heads are effective, and both have particular considerations. Fabric brush heads accumulate dirt and debris from the ice and therefore must be regularly cleaned or replaced when they wear out. Some of the materials used for

Figure 9 Brushes: *(a)* cloth-covered head; *(b)* hair brush.

fabric brushes allow for simple soap and water cleaning, while others do not. Fabric brush heads, also commonly known as synthetics, are cleaner on the curling ice surface than hair brushes. Synthetic brushes work on the top of the pebble surface and are very effective at polishing that particular part of the ice.

Hair brushes have the advantage of being able to reach down between pebble and remove any frost creeping up the sides. However, not all curling surfaces experience frost, so this is not always an advantage. Another major difference between fabric and hair brushes is that hair brushes have the potential to shed their hairs. A dropped hair can have a major impact on a shot if the rock picks it up while traveling down the ice. Hair brushes must be regularly inspected to ensure that any loose hairs are removed before play.

Broom shafts are typically made from a fiberglass or carbon fiber material. The shafts need to withstand considerable downward (compression) force but do not have to withstand a great amount of bend. Carbon fiber is popular because it is considerably lighter than fiberglass and allows a brusher to apply more force to the brush head.

Many brush heads can be angled so that players can adjust how the head passes across the running path of the rock. As you will see, there is an ideal angle for the brush head to cross the path, and being able to adjust the head allows people of various sizes to maximize the effort they apply while brushing. Also, it is common to use the brush as a stabilizing device during delivery, so being able to angle the brush head allows for adjustment in the delivery.

Brushes are not the only devices used to stabilize players during their deliveries. There are currently a number of products that are used for this purpose only. They come in a variety of shapes and sizes and are used only during the delivery (figure 10).

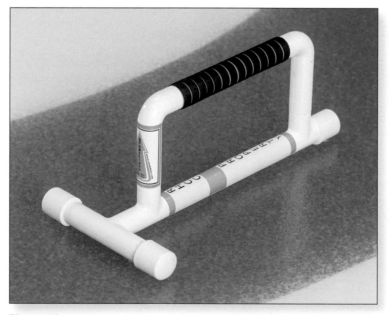

Figure 10   Delivery aid.

Apparel

Players need clothing that allows them to easily move through a full range of motion while they play. The pants curlers wear are typically made to stretch to allow players to comfortably get into the extended slide position. Upper-body wear is similarly stretchy to allow for effective sweeping. Clothing for curling is more commonly being made out of materials that wick away sweat to keep the player comfortable and warm. Conditions within a curling facility are cold, and so clothing needs to help maintain a player's body heat.

Players also need specific shoes (figure 11). In reality, any shoes will do, but the soles of the shoes must be specifically treated to allow players to slide properly. One of the two shoes a player wears will have a material that decreases the friction on that foot. The treatment of the soles depends on the handedness of the player, since a right-handed player slides on his left foot and a left-handed player slides on his right foot. Many variations of this material and its application are offered by curling shoe manufacturers. Teflon is a common material used for the slider; however, plastics, stainless steel, and even glass have been tried as sliding materials.

The slider foot is typically covered with a removable rubber gripper boot that is taken off while a player is delivering a stone. The gripper covers and protects the sliding material as well as provides a more stable surface for the player to walk on while not delivering stones. The non-sliding foot is covered with a rubber sole to add extra grip to that foot. Often a crepe-type rubber material is used for this.

Beginners typically play with clean running shoes and a removable sliding device. Once a player gains some experience and skill, it is important to get a proper pair of curling shoes because the most basic equipment does not promote higher levels of skill development. Sport-specific shoes are much better at providing a consistent sliding surface for players and allow for faster skill progression.

Figure 11   Curling shoes.

Players often wear gloves or mitts, not only to keep their hands warm during play but also to help prevent blisters or wear on the brushers' hands. Some handwear has padded areas for this purpose.

A variety of other curling equipment is available, such as knee pads, but the only essential equipment is proper clothing, a pair of appropriate shoes, and a brush.

BASIC RULES AND GAME PLAY

One of the unique aspects of curling is that it is both very much an individual sport and a team sport at the same time. A curling team consists of four players. The lead throws first; the second throws second; the vice skip, or mate, throws third; and the skip throws last. Each player throws two stones in a row, alternating with the opposition. Therefore, each team has eight stones to deliver. The process of both teams delivering all of their stones is called an end, and a curling game will have a predetermined number of ends. An end in curling is somewhat similar to an inning in baseball. The number of ends that make up the entire game usually depends on the level of competition. Olympic curling and world championship play consist of games with 10 ends, while some of the higher-level money events consist of 8 ends. Often social leagues and club games are 6 to 8 ends. While games are scheduled for a certain number of ends, one unique aspect of curling at all levels is that teams may concede their games at any time. Rules typically state that teams must concede games when they are mathematically unable to win.

Only one team scores in each end—the team with a stone on the rings closest to the center. That team scores 1 point for every stone that is closer than the opponents' closest stone. Some stones can be in play but not be eligible for scoring because they have come to rest inside the hog line but not covering a portion of the rings. In any given end, it is possible for a team to score a maximum of 8 points, though this is exceedingly rare. See figure 12 for a scoring example.

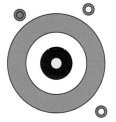

| ⊚ Red scores 1 | ◎ Yellow scores 3 | ⊚ Red scores 1 | No scores (blank end) |

Figure 12   Scoring example.

Curling is turn-based in that only one team delivers stones at a time. Because points are awarded at the conclusion of an end, the team with the last shot has an advantage. This last-rock advantage is commonly known as the hammer. In the first end of play, the hammer is determined by specific competition rules. In regular club play, this is usually a coin flip; at higher levels, last-rock advantage is usually determined by a draw to the button by both teams. Before the game starts, one player from each team throws a stone to the rings, and the team whose stone is closest to the center gets last rock in the first end. After the first end, the team that did not score gets last-rock advantage in the next end. It's possible in a curling end for neither team to score; this is called a blank end. In the event of a blank end, the last-rock advantage is maintained by the team that held it in the previously played end. Blanking an end on purpose is a tactical decision commonly used to maintain last-rock advantage further into the game.

After last-rock determination, the lead for the team without last rock delivers the first stone. Although a single person delivers the stones, each shot is completed with the help of the entire team. All four players have specific duties on every shot. The lead, second, and third deliver their stones with instructions coming from the skip at the far end. The skip lets the team know where she wants the stone to end up and what kind of shot she is looking for by indicating where to aim the stone and what rotation, or curl, to use. The other two non-delivering players on the team brush the ice in front of the stone as needed as it travels down the sheet. The skip guides the sweepers on whether brushing is needed as the shot progresses.

Once the shot comes to rest, the opposing team is then free to make their shot. When it comes time for the skip to deliver her stones, the third, or vice skip, takes over in the rings to help call the shot. The decision on what shot to make is usually made by the skip herself in collaboration with the vice skip. During the actual shot, the vice skip holds the broom and directs the sweepers. Once all 16 rocks have been delivered, the vice skips from both teams agree on the score, and play proceeds to the next end. The team that scored in the previous end takes the first shot in the following end.

ETIQUETTE

Another aspect of curling that entrances people is the tradition of sportsmanship associated with game play found throughout the sport. Even at the highest level of competition, players are expected to police themselves and to a large extent declare their own fouls during the game. There are few officials for any specific game and none at club play. Every game starts with a handshake, again even at the highest level of competition. Similarly, every game ends with another handshake. If there is any sacred tradition in curling, this is it. Not shaking hands before or after a game is a major social infraction and is considered to be extremely poor sportsmanship.

Some rules direct teams on how to behave while the opposition delivers their stones. The rule of thumb around all this is that you may not interfere directly or indirectly with the opposition while they are throwing. Observance of these rules is expected not only from the point of view of playing within the rules but also from the point of view of playing with a spirit of sportsmanship.

Although some of these matters are specifically called out in the rule book, some are not. Regardless of whether behavior is written into the rules or not, there is a high expectation that this demonstration of sportsmanship be observed.

At the club level there are other customs and traditions that all contribute to the social side of the game. These customs vary from region to region but are all founded from a spirit of inclusion.

SAFETY

At first glance, curling doesn't look like the type of activity in which injury is a large concern. But some unique game factors do create risk for players. First of these is the nature of the ice surface. Curling ice is specifically made to be as slippery as possible, and so the risk of slipping is significant, especially when you consider that players wear one shoe that is treated with something to make that shoe even more slippery than normal. Moving safely on curling ice during game play is a skill in itself. A complicating factor is the curling stones. Granite stones are heavy and just high enough to contact players above the ankle, which is an ideal place to knock a person over. Further complications are introduced during game play when multiple rocks travel in different directions; staying out of their way while keeping balanced can prove challenging, but falling is the major risk factor in the game.

Certainly the cold environment poses some risk as well, as does the physical exertion required, typical of any sport.

FITNESS

One aspect of curling that is commonly misunderstood is the fitness level required to compete. Many people are much more familiar with the social game of curling and not the competitive game, and simply watching the game leads many to the impression that minimum physical fitness is required. Although the game can be played without a high degree of fitness, in order to succeed beyond a basic level, players must train their bodies.

Certainly flexibility is a major component of the game, and players must work on their whole-body flexibility. Core strength is another major physical requirement of curlers. A strong core aids in balance and in the ability to sweep effectively. Leg strength and upper-body strength are needed for both delivery and brushing. Effective brushing does not depend solely on arm strength. One of the most critical physical fitness requirements is aerobic endurance. Curling is a precision game with a high degree of physical exertion built in. During their delivery, players must be calm and focused, and often they must get to this state after fully exerting themselves from brushing a teammate's shot. Aerobic health is essential in order for the heart rate to come down quickly enough to allow for accuracy during the delivery. Competitive players today work hard to build aerobic fitness, with interval training a high priority. If there is another sport to compare this to, it is the biathlon where competitors are required to cross-country ski to a destination and then shoot at a target as quickly and accurately as possible. In this sense, curling is very similar.

Warm-Up

Curling is physical. There is no getting around this fact. Historically the fitness requirement of curling has not been given its due attention, but that has changed in today's game. Today's top teams train year round in order to be able to compete to the best of their ability, and this sets a good example for players and teams just starting out. You may not be aiming for the Olympics, but attention to fitness can extend your curling career regardless of your playing level. If you intend to pursue a competitive career in curling, you should make fitness training a priority.

Regardless of your aspirations, everyone who curls should get into the habit of warming up before games and practices and cooling down properly when finished. The benefits of both the warm-up and cool-down are well worth the relatively short time investment.

A proper warm-up for curling consists of three stages, each graduating to the next and each with its own purpose in preparing you for activity.

1. **Aerobic preparation.** The first step is to activate your circulatory system with some general light physical activity. Possible activities are running on the spot, jumping jacks, or even some spirited dancing. The activity should not leave you breathless, as it is not a workout; you want just enough activity to elevate your heart rate slightly and prepare your body for more activity. This should not last more than five minutes and should not be so intense that you break a sweat. The aerobic preparation should take place off the ice in a warm lounge or change room.

2. **Stretching.** Dynamic stretching prepares the various muscle groups about to be used. Dynamic stretches involve moving through a range of motion. Examples include walking lunges, leg swings, and torso twists. Dynamic stretches should not extend past a comfortable range and should work each major muscle group that you intend to use. In curling, this is a fairly comprehensive list of muscles that includes the upper and lower legs, arms, back, shoulders, and core. Curling is a "sided" game in that players assume very nonsymmetric positions while playing. The temptation may be to stretch only the side you think you work the most. For the best preparation, however, it is important to stretch both sides as evenly as possible. This step should last as long as required, but you should be able to stretch adequately in about 10 minutes. Stretching should also take place off the ice in the warmth of the curling facility.

3. **Sliding and brushing.** The final stage of the warm-up is to mimic the sport-specific movements you are about to perform. In curling there are two primary movements: sliding and brushing. Taking some practice slides before your game is the final activity you should perform in your pregame preparation. Full-out slides without a stone are a good preparation, but progressive slides as described in Step 5: Shots, are also a very good warm-up. These warm-up slides should take place toward the edge of the sheet from the hack rather than up the center to help preserve the playing surface. You should also attempt some medium to hard brushing partway up the side line of the sheet. This is the other major movement that your body will experience during the game, and this sport-specific action will help fully prepare both your body and mind for the game or practice ahead.

An added benefit of a proper warm-up is that it gives you and your team an opportunity to mentally prepare for the game ahead. Making your warm-up a routine that you follow before every game and practice can establish a competitive mind-set and help you focus on your upcoming tasks.

Cool-Down

Once your game or practice is over, make time for a cool-down session. The majority of the cool-down should consist of static stretching. This type of stretching will help your body process any leftover lactic acid that has built up in your muscles. Lactic acid is the cause of any soreness and stiffness you may experience. The same muscles that were warmed up should now be cooled down with static stretching. Static stretches involve pulling the muscles slowly to extend them and holding them in position for a short time. Stretches should not hurt or be performed to the extreme limits of a person's capability; rather, they should be far enough that you feel a slight pull. Proper cool-downs will improve your flexibility and your recovery. In competition you may be required to play two or more games in a single day, even at social events, and so taking the time for a proper warm-up and cool-down will help your body perform at its best in every game.

Brushing

People can be forgiven for thinking curling is nothing more than shuffleboard on ice. Certainly the playing area and method of play in both sports resemble each other at first. Even the objects of play—round discs in shuffleboard, round stones in curling—look similar. Upon deeper inspection, you'll find many obvious differences between the two sports, but perhaps the biggest and most fundamental difference is the behavior of the objects of play. In shuffleboard, the discs are propelled toward a scoring diagram marked out on the court. The disc travels down the court in a straight line unless it contacts another disc and rebounds off it. Curling stones are also propelled toward a scoring area; however, the stones take a curved path down the sheet of ice, and except in specific situations, they do not travel in a straight line. This curved path is referred to as the curl. Curl adds a dimension to game play that shuffleboard lacks, and it is described in more detail in steps 4 and 6. The impact of curl on the game cannot be overemphasized; the game literally isn't curling unless stones follow a curved path, which allows for precise placement of the rocks.

Brushing refers to using a curling brush to scrub the ice in front of a moving stone, with the intention of having a particular effect on its path. The term *brushing* is relatively new in curling and has come into the game's lexicon because of an evolution in equipment. In the sport's earlier days, straw or corn brooms were used to clear the path, so the action was more commonly known as *sweeping*. The earliest brooms were exactly what you think of when you picture a straw broom, and their purpose was to do what brooms usually do, clear debris. They eventually evolved into a more specialized version of a corn broom that was shaped differently to allow for more contact with the ice. The change in equipment allowed players to slightly warm the ice to not only clear debris but also have another significant effect on the shot, which will be examined in more detail shortly.

The evolution of sweeping eventually moved toward developing a device whose primary purpose is to heat the ice rather than simply clear debris away. Thus was born the curling brush. Today it is common to hear the terms *brush* and *broom* interchangeably for the actual equipment, and it is also common to hear the terms *brush* and *sweep* for the action performed.

PURPOSE OF BRUSHING

The act of brushing is intended to warm the ice surface and to remove any debris or frost from the path of the stone that might negatively affect its trajectory. Warming the ice has multiple effects on the stone's path. First, the heat on the ice pebble polishes the surface of the ice down the path the stone is traveling. This helps the stone travel farther down the ice than it would have if there had been no brushing. In this way, brushing can help a shot that was not given quite enough force when delivered by creating a slightly faster surface just in front of the travelling stone. The force applied to a stone during the delivery is typically known as the *weight* of the shot. The other major effect of brushing a stone's path is that it reduces the amount of curl in the stone's trajectory. In simpler terms, it keeps a stone running straighter than it would have without any brushing. Because brushing has two separate effects, the decision to brush a shot or not can be complicated. Often the two effects are in conflict with each other, and teams need to very quickly decide which effect is more important for the current shot. Balancing the relationship between the line of a shot and its weight is a key element in making an effective shot.

Many variables influence the brushing decision. First, teams must know the amount of curl in any given spot on the sheet. This factor varies not only from club to club but also from sheet to sheet and from path to path within a single sheet. The amount of curl also partially depends on the weight thrown on the stone. Typically, a shot with more force will curl less than a shot with less force. Next, curlers must understand the impact that they personally can have on a stone through brushing. Fitness levels and good brushing technique factor heavily into how much brushers can influence a stone's path. Teams must also be able to accurately assess when to brush a stone for the given effect. For example, if a stone is being brushed because it has the potential to overcurl, early brushing may keep the shot too straight, meaning the stone does not curl as much as needed to accomplish the shot. This ability to judge the timing of brushing is critical for being effective as a brusher. Because three of the four players on a curling team are required to brush shots, this is a skill that teams need to work on together.

It is the skip's responsibility to call the brushers on for line. That is, the skip watches the stone's path as it travels down the sheet of ice and determines whether or not to call brushers on to help keep the stone straighter. Skips are in the best position relative to the stones in play to make this call. Often the player throwing will call line for shots, but this player is not in an ideal position to accurately make this call, and so teams must learn to rely on their skip. Skips need to communicate effectively with the brushers down the length of the curling sheet, which can sometimes be difficult, particularly in noisy environments. Often teams develop predetermined hand signals to indicate when to brush and when not to. Of course, if a team resorts to hand signals, there is an added requirement for the brushers to keep visual contact with the person in the house calling the shot. More information regarding the responsibilities on each shot is described in step 7, Roles and Responsibilities.

Because the brushers are in the best position to gauge the speed of a shot, it falls to them to decide whether to brush for weight. This is why brushing decisions can be complicated. Two effects of the same action must be judged by different members of the team, and the net result of that action must be gauged before a final decision on brushing is made. All of this has to happen in a split second.

If a stone does not have enough energy to get to the desired location, the brushers are responsible for making this determination and brushing accordingly. Brushers need to communicate with the person in the house to let her know where they expect the stone to stop. This is important information for the skip because brushing affects a shot in two distinct ways, and often there are situations in which brushing is required for one purpose and not the other. The skip needs to understand the weight of the shot so she can determine the need to brush for line purposes. The final determination on whether brushers should get to work is made by the skip, who has a broader view of the house and the immediate game play situation. It is the skip's job to make tactical decisions on what shot result the team is striving toward. For this reason, the skip may choose to override the brushers' decision. To make good decisions, the skip and brushers need to be in constant communication during the shot.

Brushers may start brushing from wherever they wish down the length of the sheet; however, in order to be effective, they need to be able to brush as soon as the stone is released. Usually at the beginning of a shot, brushers will position themselves at about the tee line (figure 1.1*a*) in the delivering end and proceed down the sheet with the stone as the shot is delivered. Sometimes for higher-weight shots, brushers will get a head start and begin closer to the hog line (figure 1.1*b*) so they do not have to accelerate as quickly as the player delivering the stone. Brushers will never start brushing before the stone has been released by the delivering player.

Brushing is done with a partner, which complicates matters not only physically but also mentally in the decision-making process. Brushing has maximum effect when both brushers are as close to the stone as possible. This means there should be one brusher on either side of the stone during shots (figure 1.2) so that both players can get their brush heads as close to the rock as possible. Being close to the rock is important so that the warming effect on the ice isn't lost before the rock reaches the brushed ice. Brushing partners need to decide who will be on which side of the stone. One brusher also will naturally brush closer to the stone than the other, and this is another decision that has to be made before game play.

There has been a recent development regarding brushing styles that has taken over at the upper levels of competition. This method of brushing is very different than what is described here. Commonly known as directional brushing, it involves one brusher rather than two. The goal of directional brushing is to manipulate the

Figure 1.1   Initial position of brushers: (*a*) near tee line; (*b*) near hog line.

Figure 1.2 Two brushers working together.

path of the stone much more drastically than traditional brushing does. Instead of two brushers brushing completely across the face of the stone, a single brusher will brush at a more severe, almost up the slide, path on one side of the rock. This unbalanced effect on the path can then affect the slide path considerably in ways not possible with the traditional method. The rules governing what is legal in terms of brushing technique vary. Different jurisdictions govern this differently, and the sport is going through some debate as to how to handle the development. There is much debate over what extent this type of sweeping should be allowed in the game since it has the potential to have such a significant effect on shots. The details of that technique will not be described here, rather the traditional styles will be. The advanced directional sweeping still relies on the ability of athletes to effectively use their brushes to create friction, so that will be the focus of this step.

The combination of movements as well as maintaining control of the brush head while brushing can be a difficult choreography. Typically, the brushing pair will communicate with each other as well as with the skip during a shot. Usually, it is the responsibility of the second brusher, the one farthest from the stone, to look up and make visual contact with the skip in the house since the second brusher has less potential to contact the stone with the brush head. According to the rules of the game, incidental contact with the stone by the brush generally results in the rock being immediately removed from play. The precise rules are more complicated, but there are always repercussions for teams who touch stones while they are in motion.

Brushing Drill 1   Communication

Being able to clearly communicate the weight of a curling stone is one of the primary roles of brushers. The purpose of this drill is to train yourself to make weight judgements as a brusher and to communicate them clearly during the shot. For this drill, you will be the brusher. Start at the tee line at the delivering end of the sheet. Have one partner deliver a stone and another partner in the far house watch the shot as it approaches the rings. Move down the ice with the shot, and periodically call out the weight that you judge the stone to have. Make a call on weight immediately upon release, and make updated calls approximately every 5 feet (1.5 m) the stone travels. This drill can test vocal calls, hand signals, or both.

TO INCREASE DIFFICULTY

- Add a partner to brush with. Both of you must agree on the call and then brush the rock into the house to make a shot.
- Brush the stone while making weight calls.

TO DECREASE DIFFICULTY

- Use pylons to mark out five distinct points where the calls need to be made. Place one at the near hog line, three evenly spaced between the hog lines, and one at the far hog line. This visual cue will remind you when to make your calls.

Success Check

- Make five weight calls.
- The signals or calls should be clear or loud enough for the person in the far house to see or hear them clearly.

Score Your Success

Each weight call the skip clearly hears accurately is worth 1 point. The skip must acknowledge each call.

At this point, the call doesn't have to be right, they just have to make it (maximum 5 points).

Your score ___

BRUSHING TECHNIQUE

There are different stances and methods for effectively brushing stones. Some stances are more effective than others as long as the technique is done correctly. As you might expect, the more complicated stances are more effective, but they are also more difficult to master. The ultimate choice between stances is partly a matter of skill and partly a matter of team fit. Regardless of the stance used, the goal of brushing is always the same: to create heat on the ice surface in the slide path of the stone. To maximize the heat created from brushing, a player must create as much friction between the brush head and the ice as possible. Friction is created through a combination of pressure between the brush head and ice and brush head speed on the ice surface. Too little of either will reduce the overall effect and will not create enough friction or heat to warm the ice sufficiently. All the described stances are intended to create as much friction as possible on the ice surface.

Open Stance

The open stance (figure 1.3*a*) allows brushers to accompany shots down the ice while facing forward. To prepare to brush in an open stance, make sure you are wearing grippers on both feet. Position yourself so you are facing the far end of the curling sheet, with your hips square to that far end. Stand to one side of the player delivering the stone to allow room for that player to slide out of the hack. Grip the brush with your hands such that you divide the shaft of the brush into thirds. The hand closest to the stone is palm down, and the hand farthest from the stone is palm up. With the brush in this grip, place the head of the brush on the ice (figure 1.3*b*).

Figure 1.3 **OPEN-STANCE BRUSHING TECHNIQUE**

Preparation

1. Grippers on both feet
2. Hips square to far end of sheet
3. Grip divides brush shaft into thirds
4. Hand closest to stone is palm down and arm is straight; hand farthest from stone is palm up and arm is bent

Execution

1. End of brush tucked under armpit
2. Head over brush head
3. Back as flat as possible
4. Cross-country skiing footwork
5. Knees slightly bent
6. Balls of feet contact ice
7. Legs and feet push beyond hip line
8. Short, compact brush strokes in the stone's path, ideally at 45-degree angle to the running path
9. Brushing occurs across the stone's face

With the brush head on the ice, tuck the end of the brush up against your body under the armpit. This will require you to bend at the waist far enough for your head to come over the brush head. Keep the arm closest to the rock straight, and bend the other arm to maintain the grip position on the brush.

Make your way down the ice using a slide-step motion, with the knees slightly bent and the balls of the feet making contact with the ice. Your gait will be similar to that of a cross-country skier as you proceed down the ice. Your legs and feet can remain under the hips, but ideally they will push out beyond the hip line as you begin to brush.

Once you are required to start brushing, lean your body more over the shaft to ensure your head is over the brush head. Try to get your back as flat and parallel to the ice as possible. Apply pressure to the brush head using a combination of your body weight and arm movement. The lower arm maintains pressure on the shaft of the brush while the upper arm controls the motion of the brush head. The brush head should travel back and forth across the stone's path as the rock travels down the sheet (figure 1.4).

Figure 1.4 Brush in front of the stone.

Be careful to make sure you are brushing across the face of the stone. It is easy for the brush head to travel off to one side of the stone's path; that is essentially a waste of energy. To maximize the brushing effect, brush as close to the stone as possible without making contact with the stone.

Because there are two brushers on any given curling shot, brushers must learn to brush as close to each other as possible, with the brush heads close together to best take advantage of the warming effect. Brushing strokes must not finish in the slide path; this is known as dumping and has the potential to deposit debris in the stone's path. Ideally, the brush head should come off the ice either after a forward stroke or after a pull-back stroke.

MISSTEP

You are not applying sufficient pressure to the brush head while you brush.

CORRECTION

Position your head over the brush head during the brushing motion. Ensure you are up on the balls of your feet and not flat footed. Angle your body so that your back is more parallel to the ice.

The open stance is particularly effective for new players because it is the safest method of traveling down the ice while brushing. This stance also allows for easier eye-to-eye contact between brushers and the skip.

Brushing Drill 2   Open-Stance Footwork

With all brushing stances, proper movement in relation to the curling stone is essential. For this drill, position yourself at the near tee line in an open stance. Put the brush head on the ice on the center line, and brush over the center line as you proceed down the ice. Your pace should be predetermined. Practically all curling shots will take between 15 and 25 seconds to travel from the near tee line to the far tee line. Choose a pace within this window. Repeat the drill back down the sheet.

TO INCREASE DIFFICULTY

- Brush to a faster pace down the sheet.
- Have a coach or other player push a stone down the center line. Brush the path and maintain timelines.
- Work with a second brusher during the drill.
- Call out the weight as the stone travels down the ice while keeping up with the rock or your predetermined pace.

TO DECREASE DIFFICULTY

- Brush to a slower pace down the sheet.
- Eliminate the brushing motion. Simply push the brush head down the center line while maintaining pressure on it.

Success Check

- Keep your feet parallel to the center line all the way down the sheet.
- Use cross-country skiing foot movement. Stay on the balls of your feet during the entire brushing sequence.
- Divide the brush into thirds with your hands.
- Keep the brush in contact with the ice throughout the entire drill.
- Use compact brushing strokes of approximately 6 inches (15 cm) total.

Score Your Success

Score 10 points if you can maintain your footwork without slipping or missing a brush stroke. Deduct 2 points for each slip or missed brush stroke.

Your score ___

Closed Stance

There are some fundamental similarities between the open and closed brushing stances, but as expected there are some fundamental differences as well. First, as with the open stance, you should wear grippers on both feet for the closed stance (figure 1.5*a*). The grip is also the same, with the hands dividing the brush head into thirds. The hand closest to the brush head is palm down, while the hand farthest from the brush head is palm up. Hold the top third of the brush shaft against the rib cage, tight to the body. Your knees should be bent, and you should be on the balls of your feet as you position yourself to brush (figure 1.5*b*).

Figure 1.5   CLOSED-STANCE BRUSHING TECHNIQUE

Preparation

1. Grippers on both feet
2. Hips at an angle to the stone
3. Grip divides brush shaft into thirds
4. Lead hand lowest on brush shaft
5. Hand closest to stone is palm down and arm is straight; hand farthest from stone is palm up and arm is bent

Execution

1. Brush head on ice
2. End of brush held against rib cage
3. Head over brush head
4. Flat back
5. Slide-step footwork
6. Closed to stone's path down sheet
7. Knees slightly bent
8. Up on balls of feet
9. Legs move outside hip line
10. Compact brush strokes across stone's path, ideally at 45-degree angle to running path
11. Brushing occurs across the stone's face

As with the open stance, keep the lower arm straight to apply pressure to the brush head, and bend the upper arm to control the motion. Your head should be positioned directly over the brush head, with the back as flat as possible. The brushing motion should be across the stone's path in compact strokes.

Much of this seems exactly like the open stance; however, there is a fundamental difference. With the open stance, the brush shaft is across the front of the player's body, the player's hips are square to the far end of the sheet, and the feet are parallel to the stone's path. In the closed stance, the leading arm is lowest on the brush shaft and the hips are at an angle to the stone. The player is closed relative to the direction of the stone's travel down the sheet.

Another way to compare the two stances is to first get into an open stance on one side of a rock; then, without changing your grip at all, move to the opposite side of the stone. By moving to the other side and maintaining the grip, you have switched from an open stance to a closed stance.

The footwork used with the closed stance is a little more complicated since you are not directly facing the stone's path as you move. You still need to be up on the balls of your feet, but instead of a cross-country type of gait, you must use a slide-step foot motion. Ideally the legs move outside the hip line as you brush in a closed stance.

Some players want to use a slider to facilitate a smoother slide-step motion when brushing from the closed stance. This is not recommended; a slider reduces the amount of downward force the player can generate when on the slider foot. Maximum force is created when each step generates force. In addition, it is safer to use two grippers when brushing rather than a gripper and a slider, even in the closed stance.

Although more complicated than the open stance, the closed stance is more effective for generating pressure on the brush head. Correct footwork and body position are critical; mastering these aspects provides the advantage over the open-stance technique.

While brushing in the closed stance, you must still find a way to make eye contact with the player in the house as you move down the sheet. This can be difficult because of the body position relative to the direction of travel, however, communication is always critical while brushing.

Brushing Drill 3   *Closed-Stance Footwork*

For this drill, position yourself at the near tee line in a closed stance. Put the brush head on the ice on the center line, and brush over the center line as you proceed down the ice. Your pace should be predetermined. Practically all curling shots will take between 15 and 25 seconds to travel from the near tee line to the far tee line. Choose a pace within this window. Repeat the drill back down the sheet.

TO INCREASE DIFFICULTY

- Brush to a faster pace down the sheet.
- Have a coach or other player push a stone down the center line. Brush the path and maintain timelines.
- Work with a second brusher during the drill.
- Call out the weight as the stone travels down the ice.

TO DECREASE DIFFICULTY

- Brush to a slower pace down the sheet.
- Eliminate the brushing motion. Simply push the brush head down the center line while maintaining pressure on it.

Success Check

- Keep your feet angled to the center line all the way down the sheet.
- Use slide-step foot movement, and stay on the balls of your feet during the entire brushing sequence.
- Divide the brush into thirds with the hands.
- Keep the brush in contact with the ice throughout the drill.
- Use compact brushing strokes of approximately 6 inches (15 cm) total.

Score Your Success

Score 10 points if you can maintain your footwork without slipping or missing a brush stroke. Deduct 2 points for each slip or missed brush stroke.

Your score ___

Advanced Closed Stance

Slight variations in the closed stance produce even higher forces on the brush head. Before attempting the advanced methods, you must master the basic closed stance. The differences between the basic closed stance and the advanced closed stance may seem slight at first, but these minor changes have significant effects.

First, in the advanced closed stance, the leading hand is farther down toward the head of the brush. In fact, the hand should be as close to the brush head as possible while you maintain a flat back position. Hands are now approximately shoulder-width apart, and the palms are not directly pointing down and up. Instead they rotate slightly around the shaft. Your head must stay over the brush head at all times in order to maintain pressure throughout the brush movement. Finally, at least one foot must be outside the hip line at all times as you are brushing. This creates an inherently unstable position and allows you to apply the maximum amount of body weight down the shaft of the brush. This aspect of the advanced closed stance is the most difficult to master, but it is critical to the method.

The footwork in the advanced closed-stance brushing technique (figure 1.6) is in fact so difficult that it should be practiced by itself before you attempt the entire brushing technique at once. To do this, put the brush head up against the side board and get into the advanced closed-stance position. Do not move the brush; work the feet so that one foot moves outside the hip line at the conclusion of the step. The brush head should not move against the side board and should give you some support while you get used to your feet and legs moving outside the hips. As you gain more and more confidence with this footwork, you can slowly begin to reduce the pressure against the side board until you reach a point where you are no longer using it to keep you stable.

Figure 1.6   ADVANCED CLOSED-STANCE BRUSHING TECHNIQUE

Preparation

1. Grippers on both feet
2. Hips at an angle to the stone
3. Leading hand close to the brush head
4. Hands about shoulder-width apart
5. Palms rotated slightly around the brush shaft
6. Brush head on ice

Execution

1. End of brush held against rib cage
2. Head over brush head
3. Flat back
4. Slide-step footwork
5. Closed to stone's path down sheet
6. Knees slightly bent
7. Up on balls of feet
8. At least one foot outside hip line at all times
9. Maximum amount of body weight applied to brush head
10. Compact brush strokes across stone's path, ideally at 45-degree angle to running path
11. Brushing occurs across the stone's face

Brushing Drill 4 Advanced Closed-Stance Footwork

For this drill, position yourself at the near tee line in a closed stance. Put the brush head on the ice on the center line. Proceed down the sheet, brushing over the center line. Your pace should be predetermined. Practically all curling shots will take between 15 and 25 seconds to travel from the near tee line to the far tee line. Choose a pace within this window. Repeat the drill back down the sheet.

TO INCREASE DIFFICULTY

- Brush to a faster pace down the sheet.
- Have a coach or other player push a stone down the center line. Brush the path and maintain timelines.
- Work with a second brusher during the drill.
- Call out the weight as the stone travels down the ice.

TO DECREASE DIFFICULTY

- Brush to a slower pace down the sheet.
- Eliminate the brushing motion. Simply push the brush head down the center line while maintaining pressure on it.

Success Check

- Keep your feet angled to the center line all the way down the sheet.
- Use slide-step foot movement, with one foot and leg outside the hip line at all times.
- Keep the leading hand as close to the brush head as possible.
- Keep your back flat and parallel to the ice.
- Keep the brush in contact with the ice throughout the entire drill.
- Use compact brushing strokes of approximately 6 inches (15 cm) total.

Score Your Success

Score 10 points if you can maintain your footwork without slipping or missing a brush stroke. Deduct 2 points for each slip or missed brush stroke.

Your score ___

Brushing Drill 5   Weight Judgment Accuracy

Proficiency in determining when to brush is a huge factor in brushing effectiveness. For this drill, have a partner attempt to deliver a shot to the far end to a predetermined distance. For example, call the shot to stop on the tee line. Follow the stone down the sheet. At the midway point of the shot, call out where you think the rock will come to rest. Repeat the drill five times. Note that this drill only works if the thrower is close. Therefore, only draw shots should be used and counted.

TO INCREASE DIFFICULTY

- Make the weight call earlier. Never make the weight call before the point of release.
- Add a partner to brush with, and discuss the weight call together. Make the call with the input of your partner factored in.
- Brush the shot to make it to the distance called prior to delivery.

TO DECREASE DIFFICULTY

- Make the weight call later. The call must be made before the far hog line.
- Allow more leeway for the points. Attempt to call the weight within +/– 2 feet (0.6 m) for 3 points and within +/– 4 feet (1.2 m) for 2 points.

Success Check

- Use your judgement to correctly gauge the stopping point of the stone. Call out your judgement loudly at the correct point so that a person in the house could accurately hear you.

Score Your Success

The stone stops within +/– 1 foot (0.3 m) of your call = 3 points

The stone stops within +/– 2 feet (0.6 m) of your call = 2 points

Your score ___

USE OF STOPWATCHES IN BRUSHING

Stopwatches can be used to help assess how fast or slow the ice is running. Theoretically, if the time a stone takes to travel a fixed distance is known, then the speed of the rock is known. Knowing the speed of the ice can help teams assess the amount of force required to place rocks in a certain location at the far end. Effectively using stopwatches requires mastering several skills, however. First, players must be able to translate the times they record into the force (or weight) they must put on their shots. They also must be able to control the weight they put on the rock so that they can throw to the target times. Players must be able to accurately and repeatedly record the times of stones; fractions of a second mean considerable differences in weight. Finally, in some methods of timing, the particular release of the stone can lead to misleading times and therefore give teams the wrong information on the speed of the ice. Stopwatches are a tool only and must be used in conjunction with a player's experience and own judgment. They should never be the only method used to judge weight.

The method brushers use to assess weight is known as *interval timing*. Usually one brusher of the pair will time the rock as it is being delivered. Two start points are common: the back line and the tee line. The brusher starts the watch when the rock being delivered passes over the back line (or tee line) and stops it as it crosses the near hog line. Ideally once the rock stops, the team will know how fast the rock needs to be delivered to reach a set spot at the far end. Brushers can then compare this time to subsequent times on subsequent shots. For instance, if a brusher records a time from the back line to the hog line of 3.7 seconds and that rock stops on the tee line, the brusher has a baseline for how fast a shot should be delivered if you want it to stop on the tee line. If on a subsequent shot the time is 3.9 seconds, the brusher knows that the subsequent shot traveled more slowly than the previous shot and can have some confidence that it will not go as far as the previous shot.

There are many pitfalls in using this method of timing as a tool for judging weight. The release of the person delivering the shot has a huge impact on the recorded time. If a player consistently pushes or pulls the stone before release, the time is effectively meaningless for any other player on the team. If the player delivering happens to push the stone periodically, accurate times cannot be taken for that player at all. The accuracy of the player using the stopwatch is also a source of error. Brushers often wear gloves or mitts that impair the accurate use of a stopwatch, and with this method of timing, an error of a tenth of a second can be very significant, up to six feet, when translated into the weight of a shot. Other factors also affect the accuracy of the time taken. How much rotation is on a stone and how much a shot was brushed both affect the distance a stone will travel and therefore may result in misleading conclusions on weight based on time alone.

Players and teams who want to use interval timing to help gauge weight for brushing should be aware of all these effects and be critical of any times they get during games. It is best not to rely solely on this method of weight judgment but to use it as one of many indicators for brushing decisions.

Another method of using a stopwatch is to take what is known as "hog to hog" times. With this method of timing, the stopwatch is started when the rock passes over the first hog line and is stopped when it passes over the second hog line. This method does not help sweepers judge a particular shot but gives teams an idea of how fast the ice is running. The effect of the release is not a problem with hog to hog timing since a player must release the stone prior to the near hog line. Rock rotation and brushing still factor into how accurately these times translate into weight, however. The effect of mistakes are slightly smaller than with interval timing as well. This method gives a different kind of information from interval timing but can be a good way to monitor changes in ice conditions with respect to weight.

Brushing Drill 6 Stopwatch

This drill helps players relate the time they record against their own observational judgment. Place a pylon or other marker 5 feet (1.5 m) past the near hog line. Have a partner get into position to deliver a stone. Position yourself as though you are going to brush. (Note: No actual brushing will take place.) For the first five shots, time the stones from the back line to the hog line, but do not look at your watch. When the rock passes the pylon, declare your judged stop point for that particular stone. When the rock comes to rest, look at the time you recorded, and make a mental note of the time.

Repeat the process for another five shots, but this time look at the time you recorded as the stone crosses the near hog line, and use that information to aid your judgment. Once again, you must declare your judgment when the stone passes the pylon. Only the last five shots are scored.

TO INCREASE DIFFICULTY

- Move the pylon closer to the near hog line to reduce the time you have to make your judgment.
- Perform the drill with a partner and play against him. This adds more pressure and forces you to be more confident in your judgment.

TO DECREASE DIFFICULTY

- Move the pylon farther from the near hog line to add time to consider the weight.
- Allow more leeway for the points. Attempt to call the weight within +/− 2 feet (0.6 m) for 3 points and within +/− 4 feet (1.2 m) for 2 points.

Success Check

- Use your own judgment, experience, and observational skills to estimate the weight of the shot.
- Clearly declare the estimated stopping point for each stone.

Score Your Success

The stone stops within +/− 1 foot (0.3 m) of your call = 3 points

The stone stops within +/− 2 feet (0.6 m) of your call = 2 points

Your score ___

Brushing Drill 7   Keepaway

This is a team drill that combines all the brushing skills and contributes to developing brushing stamina. Players assume their normal positions, with one player delivering a stone, two players brushing, and one player in the house as a skip. After each shot, players rotate positions so that each player on the team eventually throws four shots, brushes eight shots, and is skip for four shots. The player delivering the stone attempts to make it stop in the house at the far end. The goal of the brushers is to keep the stone out of the house. The brushers must determine whether to sweep the stone to get it to go through the house or, if it is a light shot, to leave it and not sweep at all. All 16 rocks per sheet are used so each player gets to throw four shots and brush 8 for a total of a possible 12 points per player.

Success Check

- Sweepers correctly assess whether or not to brush by using their judgement.
- Brushers correctly assess if the rock can be brushed through the rings or if it is too light to make it to the house.
- Brushers start brushing early and brush hard to get heavy or close to heavy shots through the rings.
- Brushers communicate to the skip their best estimate on what the weight is for each shot.

Score Your Success

Brushers get 1 point for every shot that does not stop in the house. Throwers get 1 point for every shot they deliver that does end up in the house. Each game has a maximum of 12 points possible for each of the four players.

Your score ___

SUCCESS SUMMARY

Brushing is an integral part of the sport of curling. As your curling skills progress, you will rely more and more on the skills of your brushers to make your shots, particularly shots that require finesse. Brushing can save shots that need help staying straight or traveling farther, and more important, brushing often determines the precision of a shot. Skill as a brusher requires both raw physical power and good technique, and so learning to brush effectively will make you a more versatile and valuable player for any team. The footwork is often the most difficult part of the skill to master; however, good footwork pushes a brusher beyond average because it allows more of the body to engage in providing power. Once you learn to use your entire body to create pressure on the brush head, you will see great advances in your brushing effectiveness. Each drill has been assigned a point value so you can evaluate your progress in brushing.

Brushing Drills

1.	Communication	___ out of 10
2.	Open-Stance Footwork	___ out of 20
3.	Closed-Stance Footwork	___ out of 20
4.	Advanced Closed-Stance Footwork	___ out of 20
5.	Weight Judgment Accuracy	___ out of 15
6.	Stopwatch	___ out of 15
7.	Keepaway	___ out of 12
	Total	**___ out of 112**

A combined score of 89 or more indicates that you gained considerable proficiency as a brusher. A combined score between 72 and 88 indicates that you have gained acceptable proficiency as a brusher. A score of less than 72 indicates that you need to continue working and practicing the techniques. It is not necessary to achieve a specific score before continuing on to the next step because brushing is a separate set of skills from the delivery; however, as mentioned, brushing is critical in the sport, and once you begin playing, you will be brushing. The more you practice the techniques and the higher the score you can achieve, the better prepared you will be to perform in this area of the game.

Curling Delivery: Approach

Often people new to curling think the game is fairly simple, and at its core, it is. The objectives and main rules are straightforward and easy to understand. The concept of how to play is also simple. Teams slide rocks to a target and try to get closer to the center of that target than their opponents. There is a grace in this simplicity that attracts new people to the game. As you learn more about what is going on, however, you will discover that to play the game well isn't as simple as it first appears. This sophistication that new players discover on their journey is often what keeps them curling. There is always a new challenge to tackle, and yet you can always find a place to play the game regardless of what level you have achieved. This juxtaposition between challenges and simplicity captures the interest of people who try the sport and it keeps many in the game.

From their initial exposure to the game, it quickly becomes apparent to most new curlers that curling is a game of precision. Each end is a battle between teams to see which one can more accurately deliver their stones to the far end of the sheet. The entire game is about getting your curling stones exactly in the positions you want them on each and every shot more often than your opponents. It's not uncommon for the margin of error on any given shot to be fractions of an inch—the difference between a successful shot and an unsuccessful shot is that tight. Improving that level of precision is one of those hidden challenges that inspire players to work on their skills.

Curling is also a game of control both in the physical and strategic sense. As the person delivering the stones, you are in control of how you are going to manipulate the rocks to get them into those precise positions at the other end of the ice. Your ability to control stones is ultimately what is going to determine your success and that of your team.

Just like the rest of the game, delivering a curling stone is not as simple as it may appear. The curling delivery includes separate fundamental skills and actions that are combined to create a complete delivery. To be successful, you must understand and master each component. This step introduces some of those fundamental skills and gives you a solid foundation upon which you can build your full delivery in step 3 and then 4. For a solid and successful curling delivery, work on these steps and master the skills in the order in which they are presented. As your mastery increases, so will your ability to be more precise with your shots.

The style of curling delivery described in these steps is known as the no-lift delivery. As the name suggests, during a no-lift delivery the curling stone is not lifted off the ice at any time during the slide. Curlers have many delivery styles to choose from, but the no-lift delivery is the simplest yet has the most advantages. This delivery variation puts the least stress on the body, particularly the knees. As we progress through the steps, the advantages of the no-lift style will become more apparent.

CURLING DELIVERY OVERVIEW

To deliver a curling rock, players use the hacks at the end of the sheets to propel themselves toward the target given to them by the skip at the far end. More information on how shots are called is given in step 5, Shots, but for now, it is enough to know that the skip will place his brush on the ice as the target for the player delivering the stone to slide toward, not as a final destination for the stone.

The player sets up in the hack and proceeds to slide down the ice while balanced on her slider foot (i.e., the foot with the slippery coating on the bottom). For right-handed players, this is the left foot; and for left-handed players, it is the right. The player holds the curling stone out front in the dominant hand as she slides in a position similar to a lunge. She releases the stone when it is appropriate to do so.

Again, this sounds relatively simple. However, as you are about to see, each movement is intricate and requires close attention to detail.

SETTING UP

The foundation of any successful curling delivery is balance. Establishing good balance starts in the initial setup of the delivery. Before approaching the hack, you must get a stone from behind the throwing area and bring it out in front of the hack. At this stage, you need only bring the stone to a place where you can easily grasp it when you finalize your setup. You are about to position your body in a specific way, and having to move around to reach your rock adds the risk of changing your setup.

Debris and even frost can accumulate on the running band of curling stones during play. If left there, this material will negatively affect the stone's intended path. Debris will make stones run unpredictably, and this is definitely something you want to avoid. To remedy this, at some point before every stone is delivered, the running band must be wiped clean. This is accomplished by tilting the rock on its edge and using your hand or brush head to scrub the running surface (figure 2.1). Occasionally there will be some stubborn debris that requires extra scrubbing, but in general this cleaning process should take 10 seconds or less. Once the running surface is appropriately cleaned, it is important to brush away any debris from the area in which you set up before lowering the rock back onto its running surface. You don't want to put the stone back into the debris you just cleaned off. You can clean the stone at any point before delivery, although it can be difficult to properly align your body and maintain that alignment while wiping the rock. For this reason, players should get into the hack, clean the rock, and then get back out of the hack so they can properly line up to the target without the worry of trying to maintain their position during cleaning.

Figure 2.1   Cleaning the stone before delivery.

Once the rock is cleaned, approach the hack from behind. Place your nonslider foot, or gripper foot, into the appropriate hack. For right-handed players, this means placing the right foot into the left hack (figure 2.2a). For left-handed players, this means placing the left foot into the right hack (figure 2.2b).

There are many reasons for approaching the hack specifically from the back. The primary reason is safety. Backing in or even approaching from the side is dangerous and can lead to a player tripping. From a performance point of view, approaching the hack from the back is the best way to align yourself to the appropriate delivery path as indicated by your skip.

After balance, the second-biggest performance priority for the setup phase of the delivery is proper alignment to the intended target.

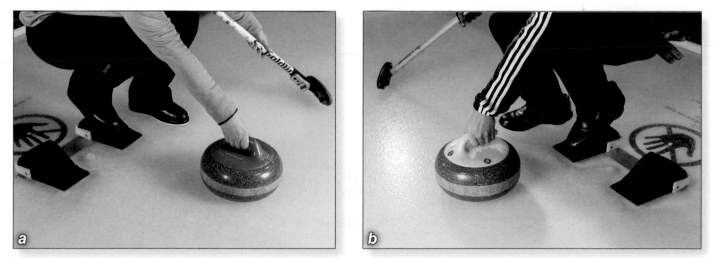

Figure 2.2   (a) Right-handed player in the hack; (b) left-handed player in the hack

To begin building proper alignment, position your gripper foot such that the ball of the foot rests up against the back of the hack, with the toes pointed toward the skip's brush. More will be explained about where the shots need to end up in step 5, Shots, but for now, ensure the gripper foot is aligned so that it is pointed at the skip's brush.

Place the slider foot parallel to the gripper foot flat on the ice. The slider foot will remain flat on the ice for the duration of the delivery. There should be a comfortable space between the feet to allow you to establish a balanced position. The precise distance between your feet depends on your body type. The key is to establish an initial balanced position, so place your feet in such a way as to evenly distribute your body weight on both. A good starting point for discovering the ideal foot position is to try to get the outsides of your feet close to under your shoulders. From there you can make any adjustments to get into the most comfortable position possible. The final distance between the feet is different for everyone, but your feet should not touch. Remember, your primary focus at this stage is to establish a solid, balanced position while keeping your alignment in mind. Maintaining balance is a fundamental skill that affects every stage of the delivery.

MISSTEP

You are unbalanced in the hack.

CORRECTION

The feet are too close together. Make sure there are at least a couple of inches between the slider foot and the gripper foot in the setup position. The feet should not be as wide as the shoulder line. When you are settled into your final setup, roughly equal weight should be distributed on both feet.

MISSTEP

You are unbalanced in the hack.

CORRECTION

Your slider foot is not flat on the ice. Make sure this foot is fully flat and that the heel of this foot is about even with the toes of your gripper foot.

Once both feet are in position, get into a crouch (figure 2.3a and b). The gripper foot should not move while you crouch. The slider foot should move forward slightly so that the heel of the slider foot is roughly even with the toe of the gripper foot. The slope of the hack necessitates this. Because the gripper foot is angled against the back of the hack, it is extremely difficult to keep the feet side by side and maintain balance once you get into the crouch position without moving the slider foot forward or without lifting the heel of the slider foot. It is important to keep the slider foot flat on the ice, so adjust that foot to the forward position. Again, both feet need to stay parallel, with the gripper foot pointing to the intended target as indicated by the skip's brush at the far end.

Figure 2.3   SETTING UP TO DELIVER THE STONE

1. Stone placed in front of hack in easy reach
2. Hack approached from behind
3. Gripper foot placed in hack
4. Toes of gripper foot pointing toward skip's brush
5. Slider foot parallel to gripper foot and flat on ice
6. Slider foot forward slightly
7. Heel of slider foot even with toes of gripper foot
8. Weight evenly distributed
9. Hips perpendicular to intended target
10. Shoulders square to target and level
11. Brush held properly to help with balance
12. Head up and eyes focused on target

MISSTEP

The slider foot is not flat on the ice. Your heel has lost contact with the ice, and the weight on your slider foot is over the ball of your foot and not over the entire foot.

CORRECTION

Check that your feet are heel to toe. That is, check to make sure the heel of your slider foot is approximately even with the toe of your gripper foot. If it isn't, move your slider foot into a position so your foot flattens on the ice.

MISSTEP

The slider foot moves to a toe-out position when you get into the crouch position.

CORRECTION

Double-check that the feet are parallel to each other. Use physical reminders to help develop the feel of this. Place brushes or other light barriers between the feet to remind you of the correct position.

USING A BRUSH OR DELIVERY AID

During the curling delivery, you will use your brush or another delivery aid to help maintain balance as you slide. By spreading out your physical width, you give your body a wider stance over which your weight can be distributed. During the slide, you may put a small amount of weight on the brush to make minor corrections, but you should never think of the brush as something to lean on. Think of using the brush in the same way a tightrope walker uses a pole to maintain balance. The majority of your body weight during the slide should be supported by your slider foot, described in more detail in step 3, Curling Delivery: Slide.

Since you use your dominant hand to grip the stone, the other hand will hold your chosen balance aid. This means a right-handed player will hold the brush in the left hand, and a left-handed player will hold the brush with the right hand. Grip the brush approximately one-third of the way up the shaft from the brush head (figure 2.4a). There are some keys to finding the precise grip location for each player, and these depend partially on individual body size and type.

Rotating the palm of your hand on the brush lets you push the shaft of the brush against the small of your back when you are crouched in the hack. Place the head of the brush on the ice so the fabric or hair portion faces up and the shaft extends out from the body at about 45 degrees. The head of the brush is approximately even with the stone in the setup. This is one key factor in determining the precise grip location on the shaft of the brush. Taller players will need to grip the brush higher up to get the head even with the stone. Press the shaft against the small of the back using a combination of the nonthrowing hand and the inside of the elbow.

Using a delivery aid other than a brush is fairly common. The grip on these devices is much simpler than for the brush. Typically, delivery aids have a handle that is parallel to the ice surface and roughly the same height as the handle of the stone. Players using such a device simply need to hold the handle and keep the device flat on the ice (figure 2.4b). The major difference between using a brush and a delivery aid is how much weight you can put on the device while you are sliding. Delivery aids allow you to lean on them considerably more than brushes, and this can be helpful for some players, particularly those with a physical reason that prevents them from supporting themselves on the slider foot. However, it can lead you to be less precise with the placement of your slider foot once you begin your slide movement. The positioning of the slider foot is a critical element in the slide. Very high-level players have used delivery aids other than a brush to slide with, but these are exceptions rather than the rule. The position of a delivery aid in the setup should mimic the position in which a player would hold a broom: somewhat out to the side of the body so that the nonthrowing arm extends to an approximately 45-degree angle from the shoulder line. This is mostly to help maintain the shoulder position, which we will establish next.

Figure 2.4*a* **HOLDING A BRUSH IN THE CROUCH**

Figure 2.4*b* **HOLDING A DELIVERY AID IN THE CROUCH**

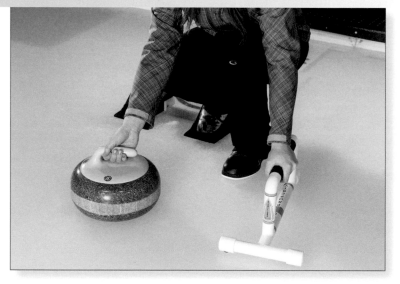

1. Stone in dominant hand
2. Brush or delivery aid in nondominant hand
3. Grip one-third up from the brush head
4. Rotated palm on brush
5. Brush shaft against the small of the back
6. Brush head on ice with fabric or hair facing up
7. Shaft extended from body at about 45 degrees
8. Brush head approximately even with stone

HIP AND SHOULDER POSITION

During the setup, you focused on maintaining your feet in a parallel position pointed toward the intended target. The parallel foot position provides a secure, balanced base, but it also squares your body to your intended target. Establishing proper alignment for the rest of the body is the next major challenge.

In the crouch position, check that your hips are perpendicular to the intended target. This is critical for getting proper line when the slide movement starts in the next phase of the delivery. To do this, check your foot placement. The slider foot should be pointed to the target, with the gripper foot parallel to it. Moving up your body from the feet, next check that the knee of the slider foot is pointing at the target, with the other knee parallel. If your feet are properly aligned, then your knees will follow. When these positions are correctly established, you should find your hips are correctly positioned perpendicular to your target.

Your shoulders should be square to the target and level. Both the position of your brush and the rock placement contribute to this. At this point, it may be necessary to adjust your grip on the brush to ensure that your shoulders remain square. This is another key to the best grip position on the brush. Players who choose to use a delivery aid may find it more difficult to keep the shoulders square to the target at this point. Because delivery aids do not extend past the hand in the same way a brush does, the shoulders will be free to rotate out of position. The brush is a much better tool to help align the shoulders during the setup. The stone should be in a position that allows your throwing arm to be slightly bent while maintaining your shoulder alignment. One shoulder should not be higher than the other in this initial setup position because uneven shoulders will cause a misalignment to your target. Your head should be up, and you should be looking down the ice at your target, focused on it.

MISSTEP

Your hips are not square to your target.

CORRECTION

Check that the gripper foot in the hack is pointing toward the target. Then check that the slider foot is parallel to the gripper foot in the setup position. Place a brush flat on the ice between your feet so that it extends toward the line of delivery. This will give you a visual indication of where your hips are aligned.

MISSTEP

One shoulder is lower than the other.

CORRECTION

Check the grip on the brush or delivery device. Your grip should promote level and square shoulders. Have a partner stand behind you and lay a brush across your shoulders to assess how level they are. With your dominant hand on the handle of the curling stone, adjust your grip on your brush or delivery device to establish a square position.

Approach Drill 1   Setup

Have a partner assess your setup position in the hack. Your partner should look for the points indicated in the Success Check section.

Success Check

- Ball of the gripper foot is against the back of the hack.
- Gripper toe points to the intended target.
- Slider foot is parallel to the gripper foot and flat on the ice.
- Heel of the slider foot is even with the toe of the gripper foot.
- Brush is held against the side of the body, tucked in with the elbow of the nonthrowing hand.

- Brush head is even with the stone.
- Hips are square to the target.
- Gripper knee points to the intended target.
- Shoulders are level and square to the target.
- Head is up with eyes on the target.

Score Your Success

Score 1 point for each item correctly positioned.

Your score ___

Approach Drill 2   Balance Check

Get into a final setup position. Have a partner lightly push your shoulders from both sides, from the front, and from the back.

Success Check

- Hips and feet should not change position when you are pushed.
- Shoulders may change position slightly.

Score Your Success

Score 1 point for every push that does not result in foot or hip movement.

Your score ___

THE PATH OF DELIVERY

When calling a shot, your skip will give you the various pieces of information needed in order to achieve the desired outcome. In the setup, the most important piece of information is the intended path the skip wants you to slide down. This is known as the path of delivery or sometimes the line of delivery. If you have set up correctly, then you should be well positioned to move down that path once you initiate your slide. The alignment at this stage is critical because once you start your movement, it is practically impossible to readjust your body down a different path. Delivering stones down the wrong path will not result in the outcomes you or your skip expect.

You have now established a balanced and aligned position from which to begin your delivery. The next critical factor to ensure you deliver down the correct path is to place the stone on that path. Perhaps the biggest benefit of the no-lift delivery is that it allows you to align the stone on the intended path right in your setup. When movement begins, the stone never has to vary from that path and can be delivered without any sideways variation. Fewer complications in a delivery mean fewer chances that something can go wrong.

While in the crouch position, place the stone directly in front of the gripper foot (figure 2.5). Try to visualize a straight line that runs down the ice from the skip's brush to your gripper foot. This line should bisect the stone in the setup and should also line up with the knee of the gripper foot. The stone should be a few inches out in front of the gripper foot to allow you to comfortably grip the stone without having to lean forward.

Figure 2.5 **CURLING STONE POSITION**

1. Balanced crouch position
2. Stone a few inches directly in front of gripper foot
3. Gripper foot points at skip's brush
4. Imaginary line would run from skip's brush to gripper foot, bisecting stone
5. Comfortable grip on stone

MISSTEP

The curling stone is not on the path of delivery.

CORRECTION

A partner can help establish that the stone is on the correct line. Alternatively, a visual aid such as a brush can be laid out, extending from the hack toward the target. The correct stone position can then be more easily visualized from the initial delivery position.

Approach Drill 3 Line of Delivery Setup

Take a long spool of string and tie one end around the neck of the stone's handle. Tie the other end around the shaft of a brush. Using four markers such as pylons or plastic cups, lay out a line of delivery that extends from the near tee line to the near hog line. Get into your setup position in the hack so that you are lined up with the progression of markers. They are identifying the desired line of delivery. Once you believe you are in position, have a partner take the brush and stand at the near hog line with the brush positioned at the last marker (figure 2.6). The goal of the drill is to have the string run overtop all the markers in the line that you expect to slide down once you have the rock set up.

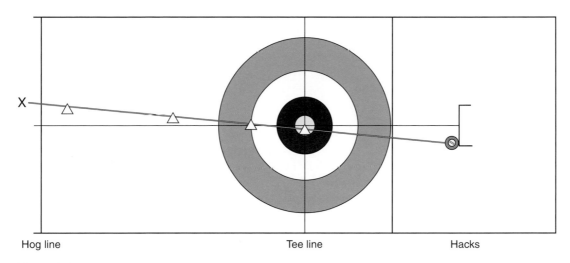

Hog line   Tee line   Hacks

Figure 2.6 Line of delivery setup drill.

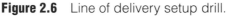

TO INCREASE DIFFICULTY

- Extend the line of markers farther down the sheet to the halfway point or to the far house. Add up to a total of 10 markers, and then position the skip's brush at the extended distance.

TO DECREASE DIFFICULTY

- Reduce the distance of the line of markers to the top of the house. Have your partner check your alignment at that distance.

Success Check

- Use the correct delivery setup. Ensure that your feet are both parallel to the string in your set up and that the stone is positioned so that the string is overtop all the markers once you're set up.

Score Your Success

Score 1 point for every marker that has the string over the top of it.

Your score ___

CURLING GRIP

Establishing a proper grip in the approach is essential for having a proper release later in the curling delivery. The proper release is discussed in step 4, Curling Delivery: Release and Turns, but it cannot be accomplished without the proper grip. Often, players wear gloves or mitts to keep their hands warm and to help with physical wear and tear on their hands while brushing. Always remove any handwear before delivering your stone. You cannot get a proper grip with mitts or gloves, and as you will see later on, it is very difficult to establish a good feel for shots or achieve a clean release unless you grip the handle with your bare hand.

The fingers of the gripping hand (right for right-handed players, left for left-handed players) should wrap under the handle of the stone (figure 2.7). There should be no space between those four fingers. The second pad of the fingers should contact the bottom of the handle, with the majority of the pressure on the first two fingers. From this position, the thumb then wraps around the handle so that the inside edge of the thumb is pressed against the side of the handle.

Figure 2.7 **GRIP ON THE STONE**

1. Bare hands
2. Fingers wrapped under handle with pressure on second pad of the fingers
3. Fingers tight together
4. Thumb wrapped around handle
5. Wrist high
6. Arm extended slightly to final position
7. Slight bend in elbow
8. Shoulders level

Most of the grip on the stone comes from the pressure applied by the ring formed by the index finger and the thumb. Although the other fingers are in contact with the handle, control is maintained by the index finger and thumb combination. If you have the correct grip, your wrist should be fairly high.

MISSTEP

Your fingers are splayed open along the length of the curling handle.

CORRECTION

Tighten the fingers together so there is no space between them. Athletic tape can be used to tape the fingers lightly together to help establish this form.

Once the grip has been established, the arm should be extended slightly to the final position. There should be a slight bend in the elbow of the throwing arm, but the arm should not be excessively loose or rigid.

MISSTEP

Your shoulders lose their position when you grip the stone. One shoulder droops relative to the other.

CORRECTION

Check the grip on the stone to make sure it is correct. Move the stone closer to the body or farther as needed to reestablish level shoulders. Once you find a comfortable position, double-check the hand position on the brush or delivery aid to make sure no corrections are required on that side of the body.

Approach Drill 4   Grip Check

Establish a line of delivery for setup. This can be a partner holding a brush at the near tee line or a pylon used as a target. Get into your setup position with your correct grip and rock placement. Have a partner or coach evaluate your setup using the Success Check.

Success Check

- Rock is bisected by the straight imaginary line between the target, the gripper foot, and the knee of the gripper-foot leg.
- Fingers are wrapped around the handle of the stone.
- Thumb is around the opposite side of the handle and curled around it.
- All fingers are touching each other on the throwing hand.
- Palm of the hand is not resting on the top of the curling rock handle.
- Wrist is high over the stone.

Score Your Success

Score 1 point for each item correctly positioned.

Your score ___

SUCCESS SUMMARY

Your journey toward making successful and precise shots starts with strong delivery fundamentals. It also begins with how you set up in the hack at the very outset. Players cannot simply stand in the hack and begin movement without establishing balance and alignment. The movement in the delivery is an extension of what you have built in the setup phase, and so any errors in that setup will only get worse once you initiate movement.

Establishing both good balance and proper alignment is essential before players can move to the next phase of the delivery. As you learn about the next phases, you will see that the emphasis on these two critical factors does not diminish—they are keys to successful shot making. As you learn to throw the various shots required in the game, mastering this initial approach will give you the fundamental skills you need in order to slide, setting you up for a solid delivery.

Each drill has been assigned a point value so you can evaluate your progress in the approach.

Approach Drills

1. Setup   ___ out of 10

2. Balance Check   ___ out of 4

3. Line of Delivery Setup   ___ out of 4

4. Grip Check   ___ out of 6

   Total   ___ **out of 24**

A combined score of 20 or greater indicates that you are prepared to move on to meet the challenges presented in step 3. A score between 16 and 20 is considered adequate, and you can move to the next step after some additional practice. A score of less than 16 means you need to review, practice, and improve your performance in all these skills before moving to the next step.

Curling Delivery: Slide

Twice in every end you will be required to deliver a stone to the far end of the sheet. Each player therefore contributes 25 percent of her team's shots in every game. Let that sink in for a second. For one quarter of your team's game, you will be in the spotlight, making the only play happening in your game. You will certainly rely on your teammates to help make those shots with good brushing and good calls from the house; however, the stone is in your hands during those shots. For this reason, curling can feel like a very solitary team sport because when you are throwing, you are the center of attention. This can occasionally be daunting, but it is the nature of the sport. Obviously, you want to be as accurate as possible with every shot, and this will depend on how well you master your delivery. We have already started that process by getting set up properly, but we can't just sit in the hack. Now we have to move from our set up into our slide.

The delivery involves a complex set of movements. Just as you saw in step 2, Curling Delivery: Approach, the details of your body position and the accuracy of your movements all affect your shot. The precision of your movements ultimately determines the precision of your shots, so it is critical to work on gaining skill in the slide portion of your delivery.

A proper setup builds the foundation on which you can successfully propel yourself and your stone down the ice to the intended target. Both balance and alignment, which were so heavily emphasized in the last step, remain fundamentally important as you work through this phase of your delivery.

During the course of a curling game, you will be required to throw a variety of shots down different paths with different weights. More information on specific shots is given in step 5, Shots, and your ability to make different shots will depend on your mastery of the slide fundamentals. Thankfully, the fundamental skills required to successfully slide down the ice and deliver your stone do not change with respect to which type of shot you may be attempting. Delivery adjustments are required depending on the shot called, but the essential skills of proper alignment and balance do not vary from shot to shot.

As you prepare to move out of the hack, remember that the two aspects of a successful curling shot are line and the force applied to the stone, commonly called *weight*. The proper setup has given you the basis for moving down the correct line, and as movement begins, you will need to take care to maintain this line. The weight applied to the stone as you slide out is generated by the way your body moves during this phase. Initial movement from the setup in the hack occurs in a specific order, and executing movements in the proper sequence is essential not only to maintain balance and line but also to give you the best opportunity to apply the desired weight to the stone. Every stage of the slide should be practiced without a stone first. Because balance is such an important factor in the slide, it is critical that you learn to slide without a stone in a balanced position. That way, once you do put a stone in your hand you will not have to lean on it.

As we did for the setup, we will break these skills down piece by piece so you can master each individually before putting them all together into a full slide.

FORWARD PRESS

Often the first movement after the setup is a forward press. This movement is optional but does serve a number of useful functions.

Occasionally, depending on ice conditions, stones can stick to the ice if left in one spot for too long. This can happen in the amount of time it takes to get yourself into the setup position, particularly if the pebble is considerably worn in the small area in front of the hacks. Performing a forward press can help overcome that stickiness in preparation for the rest of the delivery. A sticky rock can be a problem in the first stages of the movement because it can cause a pause in the fluid motion you are trying to achieve. As you begin to move you are expecting the rock to slide, but imagine instead that it stays in its initial position. This hitch can throw off all subsequent movements and ruin your shot.

A forward press can also serve as a mental cue to help you initiate movement. As you build your delivery, you will start to build routines, and a small initial movement can aid in that process. In step 9, we discuss how a shot routine is helpful for establishing consistent delivery mechanics. In combination with the mental cue, the forward press can be a physical cue to the body that it is about to slide. This may seem minor, but again, it can help you build consistent routines and overall consistency in your movements.

The forward press (figure 3.1) is nothing more than a short forward movement of the stone toward the target along the line of delivery. This movement should be no more than 2 inches (5 cm) forward and must not vary off the line of delivery. Generally, to maintain proper shoulder alignment, you will need to shift a little of your body weight forward. However, your weight distribution should not change, and both feet should continue supporting you equally. Also, your hips and feet should not move at all when doing a forward press. Only your shoulders will be in motion, and they should move only far enough forward to accomplish the 2 inches of stone movement. This movement should be very slight and can also be accomplished by flexing the elbow slightly to push the rock forward rather than moving your shoulders. If you do flex your elbow, take care not to pull or push the stone off the line of delivery. If your elbow is pointed at the ice throughout the motion, then the stone should not move off the intended line. Also take care that you do not rotate your shoulders if you choose to use an elbow flex.

Figure 3.1 **FORWARD PRESS**

1. Stone moves forward about 2 inches (5 cm) along the line of delivery
2. Body weight shifts forward slightly
3. Weight evenly distributed over both feet
4. Hips and feet remain stationary
5. Shoulders move slightly
6. Elbow pointed to the ice

MISSTEP

The rock varies off the line of delivery during the forward press.

CORRECTION

Ensure that during the press both shoulders move forward together. If the elbow flex was used, ensure the elbow remains pointed to the ice throughout entire movement.

MISSTEP

Your head drops during the forward press, or you shift too much weight forward.

CORRECTION

Ensure that the rock is moving no more than 2 inches (5 cm) during the forward press.

Again, this movement is optional, although it can be very beneficial for developing a consistent delivery. Every player should start by learning to perform a proper forward press and discard it later only if desired.

Slide Drill 1   Forward Press

In your setup, place four plastic cups beside your stone, two on each side (figure 3.2). The cups should be just a few inches away from the stone. Perform a forward press without the rock touching any of the cups.

Figure 3.2   Cups around the rock in the forward press drill.

Success Check

- The rock does not move off the line of delivery.
- Ensure there is no twisting motion in your body, either in the shoulders or at the hips.
- Keep your elbow pointed to the ice.

Score Your Success

Start with 4 points. Lose 1 point for every cup that is displaced.

Your score ___

HIP ELEVATION

Whether you choose to perform a forward press or not, the next movement in preparation for your slide is hip elevation. This movement is exactly as the name suggests, no more and no less. To train yourself for this movement, you should start without a rock until you gain some confidence. Keep your throwing hand in the position it would need to be in to grip a rock during movement. Introduce a rock into the training when you feel confident about your form. Without moving either foot from their initial positions, raise your hips so that your back begins to flatten relative to the ice (figure 3.3). Your back does not have to be completely flat, but your hips should not be higher than your shoulders. Your grip on the rock should not change, and the rock should not move.

Figure 3.3 HIP ELEVATION

1. Hips are lifted and shift back slightly
2. Back is flat relative to the ice
3. Knees are bent
4. Head is still and facing target
5. Weight evenly distributed on both feet
6. Knee of gripper leg bent at 90 degrees or less in final position

MISSTEP

Your rock moves back toward you when you raise your hips.

CORRECTION

Restart your setup, and reposition your stone closer to you before initiating movement.

MISSTEP

Your shoulders and head rise with your hips.

CORRECTION

Check that the position of your feet has not moved. Feet should still be in a heel-to-toe position. Check that your hips are moving backward as you transition from the crouch position to the raised hip position.

Use your legs to lift the bottom part of the body. Both knees remain bent during this phase. Your head should not move from its initial position, and you should still be facing the target. Your eyes should be on your target at all times. To keep your head in the correct position, your hips will have to move backward slightly as you raise them. This shift backward will ensure you maintain equal weight distribution on both feet, and it will also ensure that your head and shoulders do not move out of position.

MISSTEP

Your eyes do not remain on the skip's brush.

CORRECTION

Check that your hips are rising but your shoulders are not. The hips need to shift backward slightly to keep proper alignment.

MISSTEP

Your shoulders do not remain square to your target.

CORRECTION

This can happen if you lean forward when your hips rise. Ensure the brush head remains even with the stone during this movement.

Slide Drill 2   Hip Elevation

Set up in the hack with a stone in preparation to deliver. From the crouch position, perform the hip elevation and hold that position while a partner evaluates your form. This should be done once without a stone and once with a stone.

Success Check

- Achieved a stable and square stance facing the target.
- Balanced evenly on both feet.

Score Your Success

Score 1 point for each of the following, repeat once with a stone and once without:

- Eyes remain on target.
- Back flattens relative to the ice.
- Rock does not move during the body movement.
- Shoulders remain square to target.
- Feet do not move.
- Gripper knee remains bent.
- Body weight is evenly distributed between both feet, and there is no sideways movement during the hip elevation.
- Your score ___

SHOULDERS AND ROCK BACK

When you are in the flat-back position, your throwing arm should hang from the shoulder down to the stone you are gripping (figure 3.4). The arm should have a slight bend in the elbow but should not be too loose. With your back flat to the ice and your hips raised, bring the rock back toward your gripper foot. This is accomplished by bringing the shoulders back slightly in combination with a slight flex in the throwing arm. It is important to maintain a square position to the target in this phase. If only the throwing arm is used to bring the rock back, the shoulders will twist slightly, putting your body out of alignment to the target.

Figure 3.4 ROCK BACK

Flat-Back Position

1. Hips elevated
2. Throwing arm hangs down from shoulder to stone
3. Arm slightly bent

Rock Moves Back

1. Shoulders move back slightly as throwing arm is flexed
2. Rock moves back toward gripper foot until it is about 1 inch from the toe but not in contact with the foot
3. Shoulders stay square to target
4. Rock moves straight back along line of delivery
5. Slider foot remains stationary

As you pull back, ensure that the rock comes straight back along the line of delivery. The rock should not vary off the intended line as you pull it back toward your foot. The rock will move only a few inches and may lightly contact the gripper toe, although it does not need to do so. It certainly should not contact your foot with any real force. At the very most, the rock should just barely contact that foot. Your slider foot should not move at all during this particular motion, although there will likely be a slight weight shift backward as you move. This is fine as it prepares you for the next step. Once again, you should begin training this step without a stone in your hand. This will help you to focus on moving the shoulders back together rather than the rock.

MISSTEP

Your shoulders rotate and do not stay square to the target.

CORRECTION

If you are simply pulling the stone back with the throwing arm, your shoulders will rotate off the intended line. Make sure both shoulders come back slightly and the throwing arm pulls the stone as you draw

MISSTEP

Shoulder rotates when pulling back without a stone.

CORRECTION

Ensure you are moving both shoulders at once rather than pulling your throwing hand back.

MISSTEP

The rock moves sideways and off the line of delivery during the pull back.

CORRECTION

This can be caused by a shoulder rotation or a flaring of the elbow during the pull back. Keep the throwing arm loosely rigid, with a slight bend in the elbow that may flex. Ensure your throwing elbow remains pointed at the ice at all times. Make sure the movement of the stone is coming from the shoulder movement and not simply from the arm swinging backward.

SLIDER FOOT BACK

The slider foot, which started with the heel even with the toe of the gripper foot, now slides back so that the toe of the slider foot is even with the heel of the gripper foot in the hack (figure 3.5). This movement allows for more body weight to shift backward. Transferring the weight back helps you prepare for your eventual forward weight transfer and helps to increase your body speed in the slide. This means that some of your body weight must now be supported by the slider foot that has moved back.

Figure 3.5 **SLIDER FOOT BACK**

1. Slider foot slides back so toe is even with gripper-foot heel in hack
2. Weight shifts back
3. Slider foot moves back in a straight line and stays parallel to the gripper foot

4. Back remains flat
5. Eyes on target
6. Rock stays stationary

MISSTEP

The slider foot moves past the toe-to-heel position. No weight shifts to the slider foot as it moves back.

CORRECTION

Place a physical barrier such as a tissue box at the point where your slider heel should reach. Perform the pull back without contacting the tissue box.

The slider foot must move back in a straight line, remaining parallel to the gripper foot during the entire movement. There must be a slight weight shift to the slider foot during the movement, the specific amount of weight being dependent on the shot you are about to throw. Shots that require less weight require less weight transfer to the slider foot, and shots that require more weight require more weight transfer to the slider foot in this stage.

The precise distance of foot movement also depends on the weight desired for the shot. The farther back you move your slider foot, the more weight you will be able to generate. Regardless of how far back you bring it, your slider foot must always be able to support some portion of your body weight. It must not simply swing back behind you. This is best accomplished by ensuring that the entire slider foot remain flat rather than flexing such that the heel loses contact with the ice. Also, it is very important to ensure that your slider foot comes straight back and does not hook in behind the hack. This is a common mistake that causes significant errors further on in the slide motion. Your back must remain flat throughout this motion, and your eyes must stay on target. The rock should not move any farther back during this movement.

MISSTEP

The slider foot loses contact with the ice and does not remain flat on the ice.

CORRECTION

There has not been appropriate weight transferred to the slider foot. Check that you are balanced on both feet and that some body weight has shifted back behind the hack.

MISSTEP

Your hips open relative to the target, and you lose alignment with your intended line of delivery.

CORRECTION

Bring the slider foot back to parallel with the gripper foot.

If the slider foot does not come back parallel to the gripper foot, your hips will open relative to the target and you will lose alignment with your intended line of delivery. Even simply turning the toe out in this phase will cause you to twist at the hips enough to put you off the line. Have a partner stand close by and place a brush flat on the ice just beside your slider foot, with the brush head at the back boards and the shaft extending toward your feet. Brushes can be placed between your feet to ensure you aren't bringing them any closer together and along the outside of your slider foot to make sure you aren't moving that foot out from your body. During the pull back, do not contact the brush shafts.

If the slider foot hooks in behind the hack as it comes back, you will notice multiple negative effects on the slide. When the foot comes back behind the hack, the hips rotate off the line of delivery toward the left (if right-handed) or the right (if left-handed). It is very difficult to recover a proper alignment to the target from this position. As you move forward, the slider foot will have to circle around the hack in order to get under your body properly. Often, this lateral leg swing causes too much sideways momentum, and you will drift when you push off from the hack. It can also be difficult to shift your weight properly when the slider foot has to move sideways so severely, causing a loss of balance.

PARK

With the slider foot back, you will now pause slightly. The duration of this pause is very short, and it allows you to prepare for the next movement. This pause, or park, can be thought of as loading your body in the same way an archer pulls the string back on the bow. Longer loading times will help a player generate more weight if required for a particular shot, but the park should never last more than about 2 seconds. Both knees will remain bent in this stationary position and there may be a slight dropping of the hips, though not so much that your back is no longer parallel to the ice.

ROCK FORWARD

From the park position, move the stone forward along the path of delivery. During this stage, you will be moving more than just the stone and throwing arm. In fact, in order to maintain a square position to your target, your shoulders and hips need to move forward together. It is critical that the rock move forward directly on the intended line of delivery as you begin your motion. You will begin shifting your body weight forward to maintain your balance and to prepare for the next step. This movement is gradual and controlled. During this step it is important to keep the slider foot flat on the ice and to have the knee of the leg in the hack at about 90 degrees (figure 3.6). The slider foot does not move until the majority of your body weight passes over the hack. Even though you are leaning forward to start the rock movement, it is essential that you do not lose your balance during this step.

Figure 3.6 **ROCK FORWARD**

1. Shoulders and hips move forward together to propel the rock forward
2. Rock remains on the line of delivery
3. Body weight shifts forward
4. Slider foot is flat on the ice
5. Knee of leg in the hack is at 90 degrees or less
6. Balance is maintained

SLIDER FOOT FORWARD

Once the hips pass over the hack, your slider foot should begin to move to a position where it can support the majority of your body weight. This combination of movement is complicated because the weight shift happens very quickly once the foot movement starts. Therefore, it is important to make sure you are moving in the correct order and that your slider foot is in the proper position before you transition more weight to it.

The initial movement of the slider foot is parallel to the gripper foot, and your body will now lean farther forward (figure 3.7). The slider foot should move forward past the gripper foot and then merge into the slide path behind the stone. As the foot moves into position, the toes of the slider foot should turn out slightly to increase the base width of the supporting foot. This helps you maintain balance in the actual slide movement. The slider foot should not angle more than from a 12 o'clock position to a 10 o'clock position for right-handed players or from a 12 o'clock to a 2 o'clock position for left-handed players.

Figure 3.7 **SLIDER FOOT FORWARD**

Initial Movement

1. Slider foot moves parallel to gripper foot
2. Body leans forward

Slider Foot Moves Under Center of Mass

1. Slider foot moves past gripper foot
2. Slider foot merges into slide path behind stone

3. Toes of slider foot turn out slightly
4. Weight shifts onto slider foot
5. Hips drop down to final slide position
6. Arm holding stone is extended in front, elbow slightly bent and pointing toward ice
7. Wrist is over the top of the stone

It is extremely important to get the slider foot in behind the stone and under your center of mass but no farther. This foot movement should be controlled and is not simply a matter of throwing the foot under you. The slider foot is the foundation upon which you are going to slide. If the foot goes past the balance point under you, it will cause you to wobble and will push you and the stone off the intended line of delivery. This is one area where training without a stone will help you immensely. Often, new players will not be precise enough with their slider foot placement as they push off and so will instinctively lean on the stone as they push out. Removing the stone in training forces you to get your slider foot under you before pushing off from the hack.

The weight shift to your slider foot is gradual and continues as you move forward. However, all your weight should be transitioned to that foot before your gripper foot kicks out from the hack. At this point, your movement forward should be a result of the weight shift forward along the path of delivery rather than from a leg extension.

As the slider foot moves into position under your body, and the leg in the hack begins to extend, your hips will begin to drop down to their final slide position. This should put you into an aligned and balanced position for the leg drive.

The arm holding the stone should be extended in front of you with a slight bend in the elbow. The elbow of the throwing arm should be pointed to the ice. As through the entire delivery, it is essential to keep the stone on its intended path. The imaginary line that you visualized from the skip's brush through to your gripper foot in the hack should continue to bisect the stone as you begin your movement out of the hack. Keeping the elbow pointed to the ice ensures that any movement at the elbow joint maintains the arm and stone alignment toward the target. If your elbow flares out, you risk putting lateral force on the stone, causing it to push off your desired line. Your grip on the stone should not shift throughout any of the motion, and you should not lean on the stone as you slide. Your wrist should be high over the top of the stone.

The grip and release of the stone are explained in detail in the next step. For now it is enough to know that the precise stone grip should be held until near release.

The arm holding the brush or delivery aid should be slightly bent, and the brush head should remain even with the stone throughout the slide movement. Body weight may be applied to the brush, but it should be minimal. The majority of your body weight must be supported by the slider foot positioned under the center of your body mass. The brush handle should be pressed into the small of your back, and your hand position on the brush shaft should be such that your shoulders remain square to your slide path.

LEG DRIVE

As the slider foot moves into the final supporting position, the other leg begins to straighten out and the gripper foot will be in position to push against the hack (figure 3.8a). The force created by the leg extension is the leg drive that provides the power to propel you and the stone into your slide (figure 3.8b). The leg drive is responsible for the majority of the force applied to the stone to accomplish your shot. This is an important point to keep in mind because initially your impulse may be to push the stone with your arm to give it the weight you need. Pushing the stone with your arm does not allow you to control either line or weight, both of which you need in order to be successful. Again, by training at this stage without a stone, you will learn to modulate your weight through your leg drive rather than by pushing the stone upon release.

Figure 3.8 **LEG DRIVE**

Preparation

1. Slider foot in final supporting position
2. Gripper foot ready to push against the hack
3. Gripper foot points to target

Execution

1. Gripper foot turns over so top of foot slides on ice
2. Driving leg extends back in line with the line of delivery
3. Hips aligned to target

Many new curlers do not properly associate the leg drive with the shot's weight. Often they will propel themselves out of the hack with indiscriminant force and then shove the stone down the ice. This will not yield consistent line or weight results. The leg drive provides the majority of the force required to propel you and the stone down the ice by using the largest muscles in the body. Arm movements at the point of release are used to provide some fine tuning for weight, but those movements should not provide the bulk of the force applied.

The timing of the leg drive is critical. Early leg drive may cause you to lose balance and push off line, particularly if your slider foot is not in position to take your body weight. If your leg drive comes too late, then your trailing leg will already have extended too far to generate enough force to accomplish the shot you are trying to make. The gripper foot, which was pointing to the target during the setup and initial movement, should remain pointed to the target until it pushes off the hack. The gripper foot then turns over as you push off so that the top of the foot slides along the ice. The drive leg extends out behind you in line with the line of delivery as you begin the slide. Once the trailing foot has left the hack, it must either trail straight back behind you (figure 3.9a) or with the toe turned into the body (figure 3.9b). These foot positions ensure that you maintain your hip alignment to the target. Letting the trailing foot drag behind you with the toe out opens your hips and aligns them away from the target. The foot also acts as a rudder, pulling your entire body off your intended line.

Figure 3.9 Foot positions during the leg drive: (*a*) foot trails straight back; (*b*) foot is turned into the body.

The knee of the trailing leg should not be resting on the ice. The knee may come into contact with the ice as you slide, but it should not be supporting any of your body weight. Your body will be supported in this slide position by three points:

1. Slider foot under your body
2. Brush or sliding aid
3. Trailing foot

Slide Drill 3 Sequence

Once you are set up in the hack to take your shot, perform the correct sequence of movements in the correct order. Include the forward press. The order of the steps is as follows:

1. Forward press
2. Hip elevation
3. Shoulders and rock back
4. Slider foot back
5. Park
6. Shoulders and rock forward
7. Slider foot forward
8. Slide in balanced position

Success Check

- Maintain balance throughout entire movement. When sliding without a stone, this means you do not put your hand down on the ice to keep yourself from falling. With a stone, it means you do not lean on it.
- Maintain rock and body alignment throughout entire movement.

Score Your Success

Earn 1 point for performing each step, and score an additional 1 point for performing each step in the correct sequence.

Your score ___

SLIDE

In the final slide position (figure 3.10), you will have transitioned the majority of your body weight to your slider foot. It is essential for your slider foot to be under your body, ideally with the toes angled slightly out. The trailing leg is extended behind you in line with the path of delivery. Your shoulders remain square to the target, as do your hips.

Figure 3.10 **FINAL SLIDE POSITION**

1. Weight mostly on slider foot
2. Slider foot under body, toes out slightly
3. Trailing leg extends back in line with path of delivery
4. Shoulders and hips square to target
5. Brush head roughly even with stone
6. Throwing arm slightly bent, elbow pointing at ice
7. Eyes on target

MISSTEP

When using a delivery aid, you put too much weight on the aid.

CORRECTION

Try sliding to a complete stop and then letting go of the delivery aid. If your body tilts or if you fall over when you let go of the device, then you are putting too much of your weight on it. Move the device closer to your body and try again. The farther from your body the device is, the more likely that you will lean on it too much.

The arm holding your brush or delivery aid will be slightly bent and slightly out in front of you to keep the head of the brush roughly even with the stone. Your throwing arm should also be slightly bent, with your elbow pointed to the ice. The stone will be out in front of your body, on the line of delivery and leading the slider foot. During your slide you must keep your eyes on your target. It is critical that you do not use the stone as a support for any of your body weight because eventually you will be releasing the stone, and if it is a support point you will lose your balance immediately upon release. Your brush or delivery aid must support as little of your weight as possible. If all these factors are performed correctly, then your hips should be square to the target during your slide.

At first this position can be difficult to attain, and some people gravitate to using a delivery aid over a brush to make it easier. The delivery aid provides a more stable platform that you can lean on considerably while you slide, while the brush gives much less support. Delivery aids can be beneficial for players who have physical issues that prevent them from getting their balance without leaning, but often players will lean too much on the devices. Too much weight on the aid rather than on the slider foot creates imbalance, which can lead to poor positioning and a delivery that does not follow the desired line.

Your ultimate slide goal should be to be able to slide out and come to a complete stop without a stone in your hand. This is the ultimate test of balance and will ensure that you are not putting weight on the rock when you deliver. The rock is not a delivery aid, and using it as such will only frustrate you, because eventually you'll have to release the stone and it will not be able to support you at that point. Also, leaning on the stone during the delivery makes good weight control practically impossible because at the point of release you will need to push it away from you with significant force. The following drills will help you progress to the point where you will be able to slide without a stone in your hand.

Slide Drill 4   Slide Position Balance

This drill is intended to help your body safely feel the correct sliding position without the complications of the initial movement. With your slider foot uncovered, move to the side boards or back boards, and face the boards.

Crouch down and put both hands flat on the side boards. Once your hands are in a position to support you, put your slider foot under your body and extend your trailing leg as though you were actually sliding. You should be in the full slide position; the only difference is that your hands are flat on the side boards rather than holding a stone and brush. Your trailing leg should be extended out behind you. Once you are in this position, gently push yourself away from the side boards, but do not lose contact with the boards. Push yourself back and forth four times. You should not lose balance during any cycle back and forth.

TO INCREASE DIFFICULTY

- Once you have pushed away from the side boards, take your hands off the boards so that you are completely supported by your slider foot and nothing else. You must maintain balance without having your hands support you.

TO DECREASE DIFFICULTY

- Get into the slide position, but do not push yourself off the boards. Instead, simply hold the position and allow your body to find the appropriate foot position that will support you.

Success Check

- Let the slider foot support your weight.
- Position the slider foot under the center of your body mass.
- Extend the trailing leg with the foot straight out or turned in.
- The only points of contact are the hands on the side boards, slider foot on the ice, and trailing foot on the ice.

Score Your Success

Score 1 point for every push and pull accomplished without losing balance.

Your score ___

Slide Drill 5 Slide

For this drill you will need a delivery aid that is not a brush. Turn the delivery device 90 degrees so that you can grip it with both hands in front of you. Get into the hack and set up without a stone, gripping the delivery aid in front of you. Once you are set up, go through your initial movement and slide out from the hack. You may place some weight on the delivery aid in the slide position. The intent of the drill is to simulate a real slide with a little bit of comfort provided by the delivery aid. Maintain the slide position until you come to a complete stop. Repeat this drill five times.

TO INCREASE DIFFICULTY

- **Stage 1:** Instead of using a delivery aid, use two stones. Grip one stone in each hand, and do not release them. Because the stones are not physically connected, you must be more aware of your shoulder and arm positions as you slide with the pair of stones.
- **Stage 2:** Slide from the hack holding the brush as you would in an actual shot. Do not use a stone, and do not put your throwing hand on the ice at any time during the slide.

TO DECREASE DIFFICULTY

- Instead of using a delivery aid, use a brush flat on the ice across the front of your body. This will cause you to lean farther forward than you should during a real slide, but it will also give you significantly more support as you move, allowing you to find the ideal place for your slider foot in the slide.

Success Check

- The slider foot is under the body when the slide begins.
- Let the slider foot support the body weight.

Score Your Success

Score 5 points for every complete slide in which you do not lose your balance. Deduct 1 point every time you lose balance, up to 5 in each slide.

Your score ___

Slide Drill 6 Line of Delivery

Place a target brush at the near hog line near the center line. Space five plastic cups at least 1 foot (0.3 m) apart along the line of delivery defined by the brush and hack. With a stone, set up in the hack and then slide to the target brush. If you are properly aligned and sliding down the correct path, as the rock contacts each cup it should bounce straight ahead of you along the slide path and not to the side.

TO INCREASE DIFFICULTY

- Move the target brush 15 feet (4.5 m) past the hog line, and add three more plastic cups down the line.
- Move the target brush 2 feet (0.6 m) off the center line to force alignment off center.

TO DECREASE DIFFICULTY

- Move the target brush to the top of the rings, and place three cups along the line instead of five.
- Put the target brush very close to the center line.

Success Check

- Keep your shoulders and hips square, and align the slide with the defined path.
- Do not steer the stone with your arm and hands into the path.
- Keep your eyes focused on the target brush throughout the slide.

Score Your Success

Score 1 point for every cup that bounces straight ahead of you.

Your score ___

SUCCESS SUMMARY

The results you get on every curling shot will depend on how well you have mastered the fundamental skills required in the delivery. Although we have broken the slide into steps, it is not a series of discrete skills. A good slide flows from one movement to the next, but to be able to flow from step to step, you must master each skill on its own. Balance and alignment remain critical elements, but once movement is initiated the precise sequence in which you move also becomes an important factor in success. Success in curling requires precision and control, and in order for you to throw precise shots, you need to be able to move your body precisely.

One of the pitfalls that new curlers experience at this stage is simply remembering the steps involved in the slide and the correct sequence. At this stage of your skill development, it can be extremely helpful to visualize the movements within the curling slide off ice in preparation for your on-ice training. Mentally quiz yourself on the sequence of the slide. Mentally check to see if you remember the correct positions in each stage. This will help you prepare for performing those movements correctly once you get out on the ice.

Each drill has been assigned a point value so you can evaluate your progress in the slide.

Slide Drills

1. Forward Press   ___ out of 4

2. Hip Elevation   ___ out of 14

3. Sequence   ___ out of 16

4. Slide Position Balance   ___ out of 4

5. Slide   ___ out of 25

6. Line of Delivery   ___ out of 5

Total   **___ out of 68**

A combined score of 55 or more indicates that you are prepared to move on to meet the challenges outlined in step 4, Curling Delivery: Release and Turns. A score between 44 and 54 indicates that you can move on to the next step with some additional practice. A score of less than 44 means you need to review, practice, and improve your performance in all these skills before moving to the next step.

Curling Delivery: Release and Turns

Your last opportunity to affect the rock during your shot is at the release of the stone. A proper consistent release is essential for your overall success. A poor release can make it practically impossible to make any shot regardless of how well you have mastered the rest of the delivery mechanics. The release is much more than simply letting go of the stone during the slide. Many aspects of the release have to be mastered in order to achieve success in the game.

As you learned in the brushing step, when you deliver a curling stone you intentionally send it on a curved path down the sheet. This makes the curling release more dynamic than simply opening your hand to let it go. You need to apply a rotation to the stone upon release to make it curve in the desired direction. When applying the rotation, you have to do so without moving it off the line of delivery that you worked so hard to establish and maintain. There are very few instances in which curling stones are thrown with the intention of them taking a straight path. Even with those shots, however, a rotation is still applied at the point of release. The precise nature of the curved path your stone will take depends on a number of factors, only some of which are in your control. This step focuses on the release factors you control that ensure your curling shot goes precisely where you intend it to.

CURL AND ROTATION

All curling stone and ice surface combinations are different, not only with respect to speed of the ice, but also the amount of curl that can be realized on a shot. Ice pebble and rock running-surface interactions are unique, thereby creating different conditions on every sheet at every facility. Ice makers work hard to get these factors within a small window of performance so that while each sheet has its own specific characteristics, the differences are not so large that players can't adjust and use their experience and talent to make shots. Within any given facility, the weight and curl characteristics of ice and rocks are usually much closer to each other than they are between facilities. Rocks may curl more or less within a facility, and the ice may be heavier or lighter—adjusting to these differences is part of the game and an important set of skills to master.

Rocks have two separate markings on them. One indicates the sheet they belong to, and the other indicates which specific rock number they are (on any given sheet, stones are numbered from 1 to 8). Leads usually throw rocks 1 and 2, seconds throw rocks 3 and 4, thirds throw rocks 5 and 6, and skips throw rocks 7 and 8. During a game, players usually throw the same pair of rocks for the entire game because those rocks are usually matched.

Curling facilities match rocks the best they can for each sheet. This means they try to pair up rocks that are very close to having the same weight similar running surface. That pair of rocks should then behave very similarly with respect to both weight and the amount of curl. However, this is not always the case, and at higher levels teams will work to find pairings within their eight stones that they are happy with. This sort of rock matching requires a very good feel for touch and isn't something a newer player needs to be concerned with. The differences between rocks are usually very subtle, and until you reach a level where you can detect those subtle differences, the slight variations will have a minimal impact on your game play.

Recall that curling rock weights must be within a range and not a precise weight. Rocks of different weights require different levels of force in order to travel the same distance. Part of the effort of matching rocks is to find a pair whose weights are very close and so will need a consistent amount of force. The same sort of thing applies to the running surfaces of stones. Although every attempt is made to make these surfaces as uniform as possible, often each stone has minor idiosyncrasies. Differences in running surfaces make the rocks behave differently with respect to the amount of curl they will have. It is, in fact, the roughness of the running surface that is responsible for the curl in the first place.

In general, there is nothing a player can do about the rocks and ice. Therefore it is important to focus on the release and control of the stone, which you have complete control over. Still, as your skills improve you will find it helpful to understand the nature of the stones and ice and how they may vary independent of your influence.

The physics behind the curved path of a curling stone is not completely understood, although it has been the focus of a number of scientific studies across the world. What is known for certain is that a curling stone will curl in the direction it is rotated.

This means a stone rotated counterclockwise will curl from the point of release toward the left (figure 4.1a). A stone rotated clockwise will curl toward the right (figure 4.1b). This direction of curl is the same for both left-handed curlers and right-handed curlers. There are very rare instances where this does not occur, and those are usually due to poor ice conditions. Certain brushing techniques can also make a rock "back up" or "fall," that is, curl in the opposite direction that is expected.

It is important to know the terms *in-turn* and *out-turn*. These terms are confusing, but since they are in such widespread use, they need some explanation. When a right-handed curler applies a clockwise rotation, it is known as an in-turn. What makes the term confusing is that an in-turn for a left-handed curler is actually one with a counterclockwise rotation. The opposite rotations apply for the out-turn, so that an out-turn for a right-handed curler means a counterclockwise rotation, and an out-turn for a left-handed curler means a clockwise rotation. The origin of these

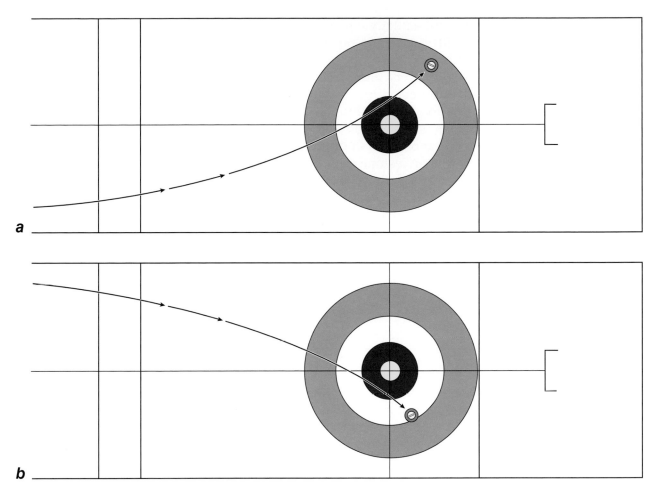

Figure 4.1   A curling stone curls in the direction it is rotated: *(a)* counterclockwise rotation and curl; *(b)* clockwise rotation and curl.

terms is unknown, but it can be helpful to think about how the end of the handle is rotated. When the end of the handle is rotated into the body, it is an in-turn. When rotated out from the body, that is an out-turn. This convention is the same for both left-handed players and right-handed players. It is much simpler to refer to clockwise and counterclockwise rotations because they are consistent between right-handed and left-handed people.

The amount of curl that can be expected on any given sheet varies and is influenced heavily by ice conditions and rocks. Part of the game is learning to read these conditions so that teams know how much curl they can expect down various slide paths on a sheet. How this factors into the game in a larger sense is explained more fully in step 5, Shots.

As a player, you are striving toward a consistent result on all your shots. By having a consistent release and being able to apply the turns consistently, you reduce the variance in your shots that are due to the release. Consistent curl for your rocks makes it easier for the skip to read the ice and predict where the shots will end up down any particular path.

To that end, it is important to apply the same amount of rotation on each shot because the speed at which your stone rotates affects how much it will curl. A stone with too little rotation will actually curl more than a stone with more rotation. At the extremes, stones with practically no rotation will lose their intended curl and may take a random path down the sheet. Stones that rotate far too much, sometimes known as spinners, will curl very little. This may sound like a strategic way to affect the path, but spinners are very difficult to control with respect to weight and are unpredictable when the rotation finally dies off. They are far too much trouble for what they might be worth. Interestingly, at the extremes, how far your shot travels is also affected by the amount of rotation put on the stone. A stone with more rotation will tend to glide farther than a stone with less rotation, even if you push out of the hack with the same drive. This is simply because a stone with more rotation has more potential energy within it than one with less rotation. The physics of curling is both complicated and fascinating. Thankfully, you don't really need to understand why things happen as much as you need to understand the effects.

For now, it is enough to know that you need to put a definite rotation on the stone on every shot and that the Goldilocks rule applies—not too much, not too little, but just the right amount. On curling club ice, this translates into between 2 1/2 and 3 1/2 rotations down the length of the sheet for a draw shot.

GRIP AND ROTATION

You will recall from step 2, Curling Delivery: Approach, that you grip your rock by curling your fingers around the bottom of the handle, with the majority of the pressure applied by the first two fingers (figure 4.2). The fingers are tight together, and your grip should be firm but not overly so. If everything is in the correct place, your wrist should be high up, roughly over the center of the stone. The grip that you worked on in that step does not change throughout your delivery and does not change with the rotation you intend to apply.

Figure 4.2   Grip on the stone.

In the setup you learned in step 2, your task was to make sure the curling stone was bisected by your line of delivery as specified by the skip. Now during your setup, you need to consider the rotation, or turn, you intend to put on the stone. To understand how to properly prepare for release, let's jump ahead to the release itself. In steps 2 and 3 you focused on making sure your body and the stone were properly aligned to the target. At the moment of release, you want to ensure that the stone is traveling precisely up that line of delivery. It makes sense, therefore, that when you release the stone, the handle should be pointing up that line (figure 4.3).

Figure 4.3   Stone handle points up the target line.

Now that you know the final stone position at the moment of release, you can go back to the setup and prepare for the rotation. To do this, you will make a slight addition to the setup. First, grip the rock properly with the handle pointed directly up the line of delivery (figure 4.4*a*), and then complete the rest of your setup. This is a good mental check to ensure proper alignment of the rock since you will have the visual aid of the handle lined up with the delivery line. Without moving the stone off the line of delivery, rotate the nose, or front, of the stone approximately 60 degrees in the opposite direction of your intended shot rotation (figure 4.4*b* and *c*).

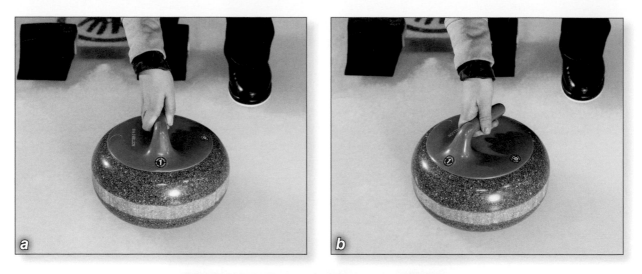

Figure 4.4   Setting up for the rotation: (*a*) handle pointed up line of delivery; (*b*) stone rotated 60 degrees in the direction for a counterclockwise rotation; and (*c*) stone rotated 60 degrees in the opposite direction for a clockwise rotation.

Another way to think about the amount of this loading rotation is to refer to a clock face. The nose of the stone is rotated from the 12 o'clock position to either the 10 o'clock or 2 o'clock position depending on which rotation you want to apply.

For both right-handed and left-handed players preparing to throw a clockwise rotation, this means the nose of the handle is rotated to the 10 o'clock position (figure 4.5*a*). If a counterclockwise rotation is required, the nose is preset to the 2 o'clock position. This rotated position is maintained for most of the slide up until about 3 feet (1 m) from the actual point of release. Only in that last 3 feet of your slide before release is the stone rotated from its initial setting to its final release point (figure 4.5*b*), the 12 o'clock position, leaving you in the handshake position (figure 4.5*c*).

Figure 4.5 **STONE ROTATION**

Slide

1. Weight on slider foot, which is under body, toes out
2. Trailing leg extended behind body
3. Shoulders and hips square to target
4. Eyes on target
5. Stone rotated in anticipation of shot rotation
6. Stone on line of delivery

Rotation

1. About 3 feet (1 m) from release point, stone is rotated to 12 o'clock position
2. Proper body alignment
3. Stone is about 12 inches (30 cm) from sliding foot

Release

1. Rock handle at 12 o'clock
2. Hand in the handshake position
3. Fingers pointing down to the ice after release

Applying the rotation over this distance is how you can ensure that you get the proper number of rotations you are striving for. There are many pitfalls in this stage, and often they combine to accumulate errors. To maintain proper body alignment, the stone should be no farther than 12 inches (30 cm) from your sliding foot from the time of your leg drive to the release. If the stone is too close to the body, your throwing arm may be bent too much and may force the elbow out from the body. This will negatively affect your line upon release and make it difficult to gauge the weight. If the stone is too far out in front of you, then your shoulders may rotate off line or you may be too low to the ice during your slide.

MISSTEP

The stone does not have enough rotation and moves off the line of delivery at the point of release.

CORRECTION

This happens if you release the stone earlier than the 12 o'clock position. This also happens if you start to apply the rotation too early in your slide. Ensure you are rotating the rock all the way to the 12 o'clock position and that you are not beginning the rotation until the last 3 feet (1 m) of your slide.

MISSTEP

The stone has too many rotations.

CORRECTION

This happens if you release the stone past the 12 o'clock position. Often this will cause your throwing arm to move sideways, throwing the stone off its intended line. This also happens if you start to apply your rotations too late in your slide. Ensure you are rotating the stone only to the 12 o'clock position and that you are not beginning the rotation until the last 3 feet (1 m) of your slide.

Release Drill 1   Tube Release

First you will need a toilet paper tube as an aid. Slip the cardboard tube over the end of the curling rock handle before your setup. Grip the stone handle around the tube. Perform the delivery as usual. At the point of release, open your hand to allow the rock to travel on its own, but do not let go of the tube; simply release enough of your grip to allow the stone to slide out of the tube. If you do not have the handle at the 12 o'clock position at the point of release, the tube will not allow the stone to slide out of your grip, indicating that you have not rotated it to the proper position. Deliver eight stones with each turn (clockwise and counterclockwise).

Success Check

- The stone is rotated to the 12 o'clock position completely at the release point.
- Open your hand only enough to let the stone slide out of the tube while maintaining a grip on the tube itself.

Score Your Success

For each release, score your performance based on this scale:

2 points: completely clean release, handle does not catch on tube, and stone flows away from you upon release

1 point: mostly clean release, minor interference between tube and stone handle

0 points: stone is not released cleanly

Your score ___

Release Drill 2   Doweling Attachment

This is another method to help you learn the proper angles for the curling rock handle. Attach a short piece of wood doweling to the top of the handle so it is aligned with the handle. The doweling should be long enough for you to see it in your peripheral vision as you slide. Slide normally and note where the doweling is pointed at the moment of release. If it is not at the 12 o'clock position, adjust your release so that the rock does turn all the way to 12 o'clock. Deliver eight stones with each turn (clockwise and counterclockwise).

Success Check

- Your release is smooth and clean, with ideal rotation to get the nose of the stone to the 12 o'clock position upon release.
- Your delivering hand is in the handshake position, with your fingers pointed up the sheet upon release.

Score Your Success

For each release, score your performance based on this scale:

2 points: end of the dowel gets to the 12 o'clock position at release

1 point: dowel is in sight but not quite at 12 o'clock or is slightly past 12 o'clock upon release

0 points: end of the dowel is outside the field of view upon release

Your score ___

Release Drill 3   Follow Me

A partner stands at the side of the sheet with a glove or mitt in each hand and follows you as you slide. Your partner should drop the first mitt on the side of the sheet at the distance from the hack where you began your rotation. Your partner should drop the other mitt at the distance where you actually released the stone. This distance should be approximately 3 feet (1 m). If it is longer, you know you need to shorten up your rotation application. Deliver eight stones with draw weight with each turn (clockwise and counterclockwise).

Success Check

- Count your rotations on each shot, and ensure you are getting 2 1/2 to 3 1/2 complete rotations on your shot down the entire length of the sheet.
- Your hand is in the handshake position upon release.
- Release the rock at a consistent distance from the hog line.

Score Your Success

For each release, score your performance based on this scale:

2 points for a release distance of 3 feet +/− 2 inches (1 m +/− 5 cm)

1 point for a release distance of 3 feet +/− 4 inches (1 m +/− 10 cm)

0 points for a release distance outside of 3 feet +/− 6 inches (1 m +/− 15 cm)

Your score ___

Release Drill 4   Rotation

Place a brush on the edge of the sheet so the brush is pointing down the sheet and the head of the brush is at your intended release point. Deliver a rock, beginning the rotation when the stone reaches the near end of the brush. Release the stone when it reaches the brush head. Count the number of rotations your stone takes down the ice. Deliver eight stones with draw weight with each turn (clockwise and counterclockwise).

Success Check

- Do not rotate the stone before it reaches the brush.
- Release the stone at the 12 o'clock position.
- Release the stone when you reach the brush head.
- The stone has 2 1/2 to 3 1/2 rotations during the shot.

Score Your Success

For each release, score your performance based on this scale:

2 points for each shot that has 2 1/2 to 3 1/2 rotations

1 point for each shot that has 2 to 4 complete rotations

0 points for any shot that has fewer than 2 rotations or more than 4 rotations

Your score ___

RELEASE

When you release the stone (figure 4.6), remove your fingers and thumb from the handle as simultaneously as possible once the rotation reaches the 12 o'clock position. This smooth motion allows the stone to flow out of your hand at the appropriate time. Relax your grip without popping your hand off the handle of the stone. This should be fairly straightforward as long as you were not gripping the stone too tightly. Overgripping the stone makes it difficult to release it smoothly. However, your grip must be tight enough for you to control the stone throughout the delivery and apply rotation. You cannot simply let the rock drift away without directing it properly or you risk an inconsistent rotation and possibly a deviation off the line of delivery. Your throwing arm should be slightly bent throughout the slide and release and should not rise up after the release.

Figure 4.6   STONE RELEASE

Release

1. Fingers and thumb leave handle simultaneously
2. Stone at 12 o'clock position
3. Stone flows out of hand
4. Throwing arm is slightly bent

Follow-Through

1. Throwing arm does not rise after release
2. Throwing hand is same height from ice as when holding stone
3. Throwing hand in handshake position, fingers closed and pointed toward ice
4. Slide position maintained

Once the rock has left your grip, your hand should be the same height from the ice as it was when you were holding the stone. Your hand should be in a handshake position, meaning your fingers are close together, with the V between your thumb and forefinger pointing to the shoulder of your throwing hand. Keeping the fingers together as you release the stone is important; if you allow your fingers to splay along the handle, the last fingers will tend to be the last contact on the stone. Often this contact will push the end of the handle and send the stone off line.

In the handshake position, your fingers should be pointed slightly down toward the ice and not straight ahead or up. Again, raising your hand and arm upon release tends to add unnecessary motion at the critical point of release. The handshake position should be held until the stone is at least 3 feet (1 m) away from you. There is no rush for you to get up out of the slide position or to change your hand position. Doing so prematurely causes you to hurry the final motions in the release and ruin your shot. Keep in mind at the conclusion of your shot that you should minimize body contact with the ice to prevent creating a hot spot that will negatively affect the playing surface.

In the release, much the same as with the rest of the delivery, simplicity and efficiency are your goals. Move only as much as is required to accomplish your shot and no more. Adding extra motion that does not contribute to the mechanics of delivering the stone only introduces the potential for error.

Once you have mastered the basics of the release, you can start to introduce a small arm extension at the moment of release. The extension helps ensure that the rotation is definite and appropriate, but there are some pitfalls associated with its addition. An exaggerated extension that is faster than body speed will add weight to the rock beyond what you have generated with your leg drive. A slower extension will pull on the stone and bleed weight out of the stone. Judging the effect of either the added weight or the pull can be very difficult, particularly for a newer curler. These effects can make all the difference in your shot. As you are learning the proper release, work on extending at the same rate as your body speed or not extending at all. Once you have gained experience with your weight judgment and control, you can then begin to experiment with the arm extension.

Another potential pitfall of introducing extension is the possibility of adding some sideways motion off the line of delivery. Remember that previously your arm was positioned so your elbow pointed down toward the ice. Maintaining this position in the release and subsequent extension will ensure that you do not push the rock sideways upon release. With the elbow pointed down, the extension will be in line with the slide path.

It is also important to avoid any movement at your shoulders. You may be tempted to push the stone from the shoulder, but doing this will cause a rotation in your upper body that will likely push your stone off its intended path. You should add the extension only once you have fully mastered the rest of the release mechanics. Even then, add the extension carefully. There are many potential mistakes in this movement that can ruin your shot, but adding the extension can help you fine-tune your weight control, an essential curling skill.

Release Drill 5   Arm Release

Position yourself across the sheet from a partner. Squat down and grip your stone correctly. Decide which rotation you are going to put on the stone and preset the handle at the appropriate angle. With your arm only, push the stone across the sheet to your partner while applying the correct rotation. Upon release, ensure that your hand ends up in the 12 o'clock position. Repeat the drill eight times, alternating the chosen rotational direction on each subsequent throw.

Success Check

- Grip the stone correctly.
- Preset the angle of the stone correctly for the chosen rotation.
- When the stone is released, it rotates in the correct direction.
- After release, your hand is in the handshake position.
- The stone rotates 1 to 2 rotations across the width of the sheet.

Score Your Success

Score 1 point for meeting each of the success check criteria. Repeat the drill eight times, earning a possible 5 points per throw.

Your score ___

RELEASE POINT

The rules state that the rock must be released before it reaches the near hog line. Your release point, obviously, should be before that line. The longer you can hold on to the stone while maintaining your slide speed, the more likely you are to deliver down a straight line; you do not want to be in a rush to release your stone. You also do not want to risk crossing the hog line, so the ideal release point is somewhere comfortably near the line.

The release point is the distance from the hack that you release the stone, and consistency is important. The rock will begin its curl and therefore its curved path at the moment of release, so if you are releasing the stone at various distances from the hog line, it will curl differently off the same initial line. A rock released earlier will have more distance to curl, so teams should work toward having a consistent release point to further help the skip read the ice. That way, the skip can have some assurance that the stone behaved as it did because of the ice conditions rather than because of the release (see figure 4.7).

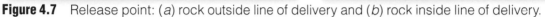

Figure 4.7 Release point: (*a*) rock outside line of delivery and (*b*) rock inside line of delivery.

Release Drill 6   Release Point Consistency

Have a partner watch along the side of the sheet. The goal is to release all your shots at the same distance from the hack within a 6-inch (15 cm) window. Have your partner use a marker such as a plastic cup to indicate the point of release on each shot. Deliver your first shot as a benchmark. Deliver six more shots, putting a clockwise rotation on each one. Deliver six more shots with a counterclockwise rotation. Do not reset the benchmark shot when you switch from one turn to the other. Your release point does not depend on the turn. Note that these should all be draw shots.

TO INCREASE DIFFICULTY

- Narrow the window of allowed release to 3 inches (7.5 cm).

TO DECREASE DIFFICULTY

- Open the window of allowed release to 12 inches (30 cm).

Success Check

- Release the stone smoothly, with your hand ending up in the handshake position at 12 o'clock.
- Release the stone within the allowable window.
- Begin your turn approximately 3 feet (1 m) before the intended release point.

Score Your Success

Score 1 point for every shot you release within 6 inches (15 cm) of the benchmark.

Your score ___

SUCCESS SUMMARY

It's been said that if you have a million-dollar slide and a two-cent release, you have a two-cent delivery (Bill Tschirhart, "When Push Comes to Shove," January 22, 2013, http://truenorthbill.blogspot.ca/2013/01when-push-comes-to-shove.html). The importance of the last set of motions on your curling stone cannot be overemphasized. The release is complex, requiring fine motor skills and touch, far different from the larger muscles used to generate power in the slide. Players often find the gross motor skills needed for the slide to be relatively easy compared with the skills required to achieve a clean and positive release. Releasing the stone seems deceptively easy; after all, you just let go, except that you don't! Although you may be able to simply let the stone out of your grasp during the slide, ensuring that it travels where you want takes more work and attention to detail.

The effect that the release has on shots is often underestimated even by experienced players. Sometimes players blame ice conditions or stones for shots that do not behave as expected. In the majority of instances, the actual fault is in the release. Pay careful attention to this set of skills. It is also important to note that the skill development has been laid out for you in a very specific order. It will do you no good at all to try perfecting your release if you still have not attained proficiency in the setup and slide. This step assumes that you have been following the correct skill progression and that you are ready to work on developing this portion of your delivery.

Each drill has been assigned a point value so you can evaluate your progress in the slide.

Release Drills

1. Tube Release   ___ out of 32
2. Doweling Attachment   ___ out of 32
3. Follow Me   ___ out of 32
4. Rotation   ___ out of 32
5. Arm Release   ___ out of 40
6. Release Point Consistency   ___ out of 12

Your total   **___ out of 180**

A combined score of 144 or more indicates that you are prepared to move on to meet the challenges outlined in step 5. A score between 117 and 143 indicates that you can move on to the next step with some additional practice. A score of less than 117 means that you need to review, practice, and improve your performance in all these skills before moving to the next step.

Shots

Now that you have gained some proficiency in the technique for delivering a curling stone, the natural next step is to apply that ability toward making shots. Before embarking on that particular skill development, you need to understand the various shots used in a curling game and how they are employed. A curling shot has many dimensions, two of the most prominent being the line and the weight you are being asked to throw. Shots are primarily classified by the weight required to make them, and it should be clear by now that having good weight control is one of the most critical skills you can develop once you have learned your delivery fundamentals. Your ability to throw down the proper line is also extremely important, but to a certain degree, good weight control can help an imperfect line, whereas good line will never fix poor weight control.

This step discusses how shots are called during curling games, weight control and line, the common shots used in curling, and what those shots are intended to achieve. Drills throughout the step will help you develop your skills for making these shots consistently. To call the most appropriate shot in a game situation, you will need to learn more about curling strategy. More detail regarding strategy is discussed in a later step, so only the basics of each shot are described here.

CALLING SHOTS

During a curling game, it is the skip's responsibility to call out which shot the team will throw. Shot calling requires a complex set of decisions that the skip has to make fairly quickly. You will see how that process works later in step 8 on strategy, but for now it is important to simply understand the mechanics of the shot call.

First, as the skip, you will indicate the desired final location of the stone about to be thrown. More simply put, you will indicate the intended result for the shot you are calling. If you want the rock to stop in the rings, you will tap the ice to show precisely where you want the rock. If you want it to stop in front of the rings, you may simply point to the spot with your brush. A shot that is intended to hit or take out another stone is usually indicated by pointing out the stone to be removed and then waving the brush out toward the back of the house. These are all simply conventions, however, and each team may come up with their own signals. Of course, as the skip you can also verbally indicate the shot that is acceptable, but curling environments are usually quite loud, and so a clear system of visual signals should be established for calling shots.

Occasionally, you will make additional gestures to show what results you are looking for. This often happens when the situation in the rings is complicated and when the desired shot is not straightforward. An example is when you want the shot to bounce off a sitting stone and then roll to another spot in the rings. In a case like this you may tap the stone to be hit and then wave your brush over toward the location where you want the shooter to come to rest. In all shots, you as the skip will use whatever appropriate gestures you can to help your players understand what you are trying to accomplish with their shots.

Once the shot result has been signaled, you as the skip will then indicate the desired weight and line for the delivery. You will place your brush on the ice to serve as the intended slide target. This is often confusing for new players because they confuse this target as the desired end result. It is not the end result; rather, it is the target line that you have chosen to have your player throw, and you will have placed it after having taken into consideration the curl of the shot about to be attempted. The weight call can come in many forms and may not be explicitly called out at all. For example, if you as the skip have indicated with your first signal down the ice that you want the rock to stop in the rings, then the desired weight is already known. Your player should know that she needs to throw just enough weight to allow the stone to come to rest in the rings. The same goes for a shot that needs to stop outside the rings. Clearly, if you want your player to put a stone short of the rings, then you need not add any additional weight information on the call. Weight calls come into play more often when takeouts or heavier shots are required. For these types of shots, a number of conventions are common. Often, you will tell your players verbally what weight is required. For example, you may call out "hack," indicating that you want the stone to have enough speed to reach the far hack.

Another common method for calling heavier weights is to use a hand signal along the arm. Typically, you will hold out your left arm and tap at some point along the length. Of course, this is meaningless unless the team has discussed what the signals mean, but commonly, a tap at the elbow means normal takeout weight (discussed later in this step). A tap above the "normal" point means more weight than what is requested, and a tap below that point means less weight. It is also common to see a skip tap his abdomen to indicate normal takeout weight. Again, using hand signals for weight is particularly helpful in noisy playing environments, but the signals must be fully understood by the team before they are put into use. There are no guarantees that a team will be following any standards. Every team must establish a common understanding of what the signals mean for their own use.

The final signal you will give as a skip is the handle required for the shot. As your experience grows, this will be less commonly required since your players will intuitively understand what rotation to put on a shot to get it to curl to the desired place. Occasionally, however, even top-level teams will need to signal the turn for the shot to be thrown. The call and application of turns can be confusing for new players, but it is an essential part of the shot, so it is important to spend some time understanding this aspect of the shot call.

When calling the shot, hold the brush as a target for the player to line up to. Remember that curling stones travel in a curved path, so this target has to take that curl into account. It is your job as skip to determine just how much you believe the stone will curl during the shot. Of course, the stone can curve toward the right or toward the left depending on the rotation applied. Stones with a clockwise rotation will curve toward the left from the skip's perspective, and stones with a counterclockwise rotation will curl toward the right. In your shot call, you will determine which rotation you want your player to apply to the stone to achieve the shot. Once you set the brush at the intended delivery line, you will then extend one hand to indicate which rotation to apply. If you extend your right hand, you are asking for a clockwise rotation. If you extend your left hand, you are asking for a counterclockwise rotation. Intuitively, this often seems backward to the player throwing, but it is the convention used by all curlers and so needs to be clearly understood. Throwing the wrong handle practically guarantees you will miss your shot.

Once you have communicated the desired result, line, weight, and handle to your player, you will stand motionless as their target until the stone is delivered.

WEIGHT CONTROL

One of the most challenging aspects in curling is throwing accurate weight. This skill is complicated for a number of reasons. First, the ice conditions will be different in every facility you play in. In fact, ice conditions will be different between sheets within the same facility. Ice makers work to make the sheets within a facility as consistent as possible, and usually the conditions are very close. However, there are always minor differences that can have a significant impact in a game that relies so much on precision. The difference in ice is manifested as a difference in both the amount of curl and weight required on various sheets. The amount of curl is simply adjusted through the line of delivery and is mainly tracked by the skip. With weight, however, it is up to the team to accurately identify the ice conditions and communicate this to each other. It is then up to each individual player to develop their skills to be able to throw precisely enough to make the required shots under varying conditions.

To be clear, when we say the weight is different on various sheets, this means that if you put a certain amount of force on your stone during your delivery and get it to stop at a certain distance, the exact same amount of force might not give you the same result on another sheet. Further, as the game proceeds, the amount of force required to place stones will change on your sheet. The ice may slow down, requiring more force to get the rock where you want it, or it may speed up, requiring less force. The only aspect of ice conditions that you can control as a player is your awareness of them. You can use brushing to help lighter shots to some extent, but there is no mechanism for you to slow down a shot that is going too fast.

Developing Precision

Another difficulty in achieving good weight control is the precision required to be successful. To put this into perspective, some shots will require you to slide a 44-pound (20 kg) curling stone a distance of 120 to 130 feet (37 to 40 m) and attempt to have it come to rest within fractions of an inch of your intended stopping point. This requires mastering the sliding technique that you have just learned as well as developing a feel for the force you are putting on your stone when you slide out. Developing a feel for weight is one of the most critical physical skills for becoming a successful curler. You have learned that fine-tuning the weight comes at the point of release, but the majority of the weight comes from your leg drive. Learning to modulate that leg drive first is essential for good weight control.

Shot Drill 1   Progressive Slides

This drill helps your body learn to drive faster or slower and gives you a sense of how much leg drive it takes to make small changes in your slide.

Get into the hack with or without a stone. Get into your setup position and then execute a slide. The goal is to slide only far enough so that when you come to rest, your slider foot is on the back line. Do not drop your trailing knee to slow down if you are going too fast. Let yourself come to a stop naturally without dragging anything. Repeat this four times with a new distance for each slide as shown here:

1. Back line
2. Near tee line
3. Top of the 12-foot circle
4. Hog line

TO INCREASE DIFFICULTY

- Add more stopping points such as the top of the 8-foot ring or a random spot past the house. Points past the hog line can also be added.

Success Check

- Maintain your delivery form in all slides. Ensure you remain balanced in every slide.
- Attempt to come to rest so that your foot is bisecting the target distance.

Score Your Success

Score 1 point every time your slider foot stops at the right distance.

Your score ___

Shot Drill 2   Interval Time

For this drill have a partner stand at the side line with a stopwatch. Get into the hack and set up with a stone. Your partner will start the stopwatch at the beginning of your slide when the stone reaches the back line and will stop the watch when the front edge of the stone reaches the hog line. The goal is to throw within these outlined time windows:

1. 3.5 to 3.7 seconds
2. 3.7 to 3.9 seconds
3. 3.9 to 4.1 seconds

Make four attempts at each time window.

TO INCREASE DIFFICULTY

- Narrow the time windows to the following: (1) 3.55 to 3.65 seconds; (2) 3.75 to 3.85 seconds; (3) 3.95 to 4.05 seconds.

TO DECREASE DIFFICULTY

- Expand the time windows to the following: (1) 3.45 to 3.75 seconds; (2) 3.65 to 3.95 seconds; (3) 3.85 to 4.15 seconds.

Success Check

- Maintain your delivery form in all your shots.
- Throw each shot without pushing the stone at release. Attempt to make your release as clean as possible.
- Make small adjustments to the leg drive during each attempt, and rely on those adjustments rather than arm movements to achieve your timing goals.

Score Your Success

Score 1 point for each slide that is within the specified time window.

Your score ___

Involving Brushers

The influence of brushers on weight should not be ignored when developing your feel. Typically, teams will work together on weight control because it is important for brushers to develop a sense of when to brush shots for weight. Players need to do individual work to attain proficiency throwing precise weights, but ultimately each shot in a game is a team shot, requiring all four players to do their jobs to ensure success. Once you believe you have a decent sense of weight, expand your weight control practices to include brushers. This helps the entire team become better at shot making.

In practice, focus on developing your personal weight. When working with your team, it should remain a priority for the team to develop good judgment of weight.

Shot Drill 3   Climb the Ladder

This drill is performed by the entire team. The skip will hold the brush as a target, and there will be two brushers brushing your shot. The goal of this drill is to throw all eight rocks progressively farther down the sheet. With your first shot, attempt to throw your stone so that it stops within a brush length past the far hog line. When the shot comes to rest, one of the brushers pulls it to the side of the sheet. Your next shot should stop within a brush length past the first shot. Continue this with eight stones. Score 1 point for each stone that you deliver within a brush handle length of the previous shot. Shots that come up short are not counted for points and do not become the new distance marker. Shots farther than a brush handle length also do not count for a point and also do not count as the new distance marker.

This drill can be a true team drill in that each player throws only two stones, rotating through the positions just like in a game. The lead throws the first two stones as the second and vice brush; the second throws the next two stones, with the lead and vice brushing; the third throws the next two, with the lead and second brushing; and the skip throws the last two stones, with the lead and second brushing. The score is then a team score instead of an individual one.

Another variation is called the progressive hog line drill. The concept is the same. The first stone thrown must cross the far hog line and come to rest. The location of that first shot now defines the new hog line. This means your next shot must travel farther than the previous shot but remain in play. Each subsequent shot becomes the new hog line, and shots that come up short of the previous shots do not score you a point. The goal is to get all eight stones in play before you reach the back line. Scoring is the same: 1 point is awarded for each successful shot. This drill can again be performed as a team drill in the same manner as Climb the Ladder.

TO INCREASE DIFFICULTY

- Use more stones. Successfully throwing 12 stones as described requires a much tighter allowable window in which to throw. Throwing 16 stones further decreases the allowable window.

TO DECREASE DIFFICULTY

- Allow a longer window for success. Instead of a brush length, allow a brush-and-a-half length for successful shots.

Success Check

- Throw weight that allows the brushers to be involved. Throw lighter rather than too heavy to ensure that brushing can be used to fine-tune the result.
- Communicate to your brushers upon release to let them know what weight you believe the stone has.

Score Your Success

Earn 1 point for each successful shot.

Your score ___

Throwing More Weight

Of course, not all shots will be required to stop in the house. An important aspect of the game is the ability to remove stones from play when necessary, usually your opponents' stones. This requires you to throw more weight than for shots intended to stop in the playing area, and that ability needs to be controlled and developed as well. At first, these takeout shots seem to be much easier, not requiring the same level of weight precision that the softer shots do. But making these shots is not simply a matter of heaving the stone down the ice as hard as you can. Higher-weight shots still curl, although less than the lighter-weight shots. The skip will gauge the target point based on the weight he expects you to throw, and without any control on the weight there is little chance of success.

Also, although the primary objective of a higher-weight shot may be to remove another stone, your skip may want your stone (called the shooter) to stay in play after making contact. Keeping rocks in play after contacting other stones increases in difficulty with the amount of weight thrown. Higher-weight shots need to hit their targets more fully to minimize the amount of roll after contact. Ultimately, while they may not require the same level of precision, takeout shots still require weight control.

From the technical perspective, throwing more weight is as simple as driving harder from the hack into the slide position. This may sound simple, but the increased leg drive can often be difficult to manage at first and can cause issues with both line and balance. Because the slider foot comes out so much faster with so much force, ensuring it gets into the proper position under the body to support you can be difficult. The faster movement can make it challenging to time your movements appropriately. Also, there is a slight but necessary sideways motion of the slider foot from the side of the hack to a position behind the stone as you progress into your slide. If this is not managed with proper movement sequence and control, it can cause you to drift when you drive out with the added weight. Fundamentals of the slide thankfully do not change regardless of the shot being thrown. Takeouts and higher-weight shots simply happen faster and with more force and therefore demand precision in your movements.

There are a number of simple ways to increase your hit weight in addition to the increased leg drive. In the setup, position your foot higher in the hack than with lower-weight shots (figure 5.1). Recall that the ball of the foot was positioned at

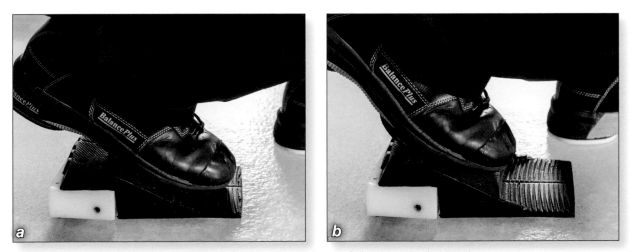

Figure 5.1   Adjusting foot position: (a) lower in the hack; (b) higher in the hack.

approximately the center of the hack in the approach. Positioning your foot slightly higher in the hack will change the angle of your drive leg as you push out, allowing you to direct more power in the direction of your target. This change needs to be slight, however. If you position your foot too high on the hack, then you will not be able to use it as backing for your foot. In the extreme case, your foot will sit on top of the hack, and you will have no backing to push off from.

Another technique for achieving more weight is to simply release the stone sooner. Ideally, regardless of the shot, you should be trying to release the stone before your body starts to slow down. The earlier you release the shot, the more initial force from the leg drive can be applied to the stone. Of course, an earlier release affects the curl, so be aware of this if you choose to use this method of increasing weight.

At the point of release, if you lower both shoulders in an exaggerated extension, this too can provide a boost of weight (figure 5.2). This method of increasing your weight can be difficult to control, however, so you should have a good feel for your weight before attempting this. By dropping both shoulders at the release, you ensure that you remain square to the target you are sliding toward. There can be a temptation to simply push the stone with the throwing arm, but this usually results in a push from the arm that puts the stone off its intended line.

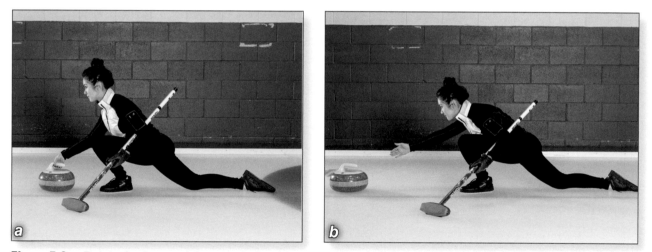

Figure 5.2:　Point of release: (*a*) normal shoulder position; (*b*) lower both shoulders during the release to boost the weight of the shot.

Shot Drill 4 Crazy Eights

Place stones of one color in the rings as shown in figure 5.3. The goal is to use the other set of stones to remove all the placed stones while keeping the shooters in play. Deliver all your stones before tallying your score.

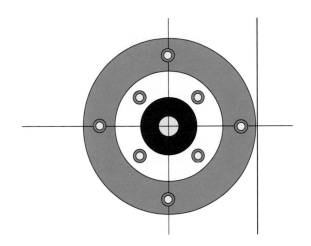

Figure 5.3 Stone placement in the rings for crazy eights.

This is most commonly used as a team drill rather than an individual drill. In the team version, each player throws two stones in the normal team rotation. Sweepers sweep when required, and the skip calls the line for the shots. Scoring is the same as for the individual version. Performing this drill as a team can help develop both the communication systems and brushing skills required in game play.

Success Check

- Ensure your line of delivery is as close to the target as possible.
- Throw appropriate takeout weight and no more. Excessive weight will make keeping the shooters in play much more difficult.
- Maintain your delivery form while throwing increased weight.

Score Your Success

After all the stones have been delivered, score 1 point for every target stone removed from play and 1 more point for every shooter that also remains in play.

Your score ___

Shot Drill 5   Insane Eights

In the Insane Eights version, the setup is the same but the goal is to remove all stones from play, including the shooters. To accomplish this, a higher hit weight is required.

Success Check

- Ensure you throw more weight so that the shooter has a better chance of rolling out.
- Ensure your line of delivery is as close to the target as possible.
- Maintain your delivery form while throwing increased weight.

Score Your Success

Score 1 point for every target stone removed and 1 point for every shooter that leaves play.

Your total ___

LINE OF DELIVERY

Throwing your shots down the right line is the next critical component in developing your overall shot-making abilities. Sliding down the proper line starts with a good understanding of what the slide path actually looks like. Being able to properly visualize the path is an important skill. Beginning curlers often don't understand that although the target can be practically anywhere across the sheet. At the throwing end, this translates into a fairly narrow range across which you will be required to slide. Figure 5.4 demonstrates this for a right-handed curler. A target variation of 12 feet (3.7 m), or the entire width of the house, results in a window of approximately 3 feet (1 m) at the throwing-end hog line and less than 2 feet (0.6 m) at the throwing-end tee line.

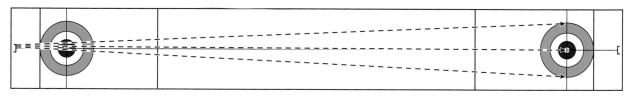

Figure 5.4   Slide window for right-handed curler.

By the time you get all the way back to the throwing hack, you can see that very slight line variations result in considerably different slide paths. We have already covered how to set up and slide toward a specific line, and now practice is required to build your skill in this regard.

Shot Drill 6   Cup Canyon

For this drill you will need eight plastic cups. Set up a target at the near hog line, and use pairs of cups as gates through which the line to the target travels. Place the first gate pair of cups on the back line, the second pair at the tee line, the third pair at the top of the 12-foot circle, and the final pair halfway between the hog line and the top of the 12-foot circle. The distance between the cups should be approximately 1.5 times the width of the stone.

Line up along the path and deliver the curling stone without touching any of the cups. Repeat this drill four times, changing the target setup each time.

TO INCREASE DIFFICULTY

- Place the gates closer together—just slightly wider than a stone for maximum difficulty.
- Place the target as wide as you would possibly need to throw rather than simply up the middle of the sheet.

TO DECREASE DIFFICULTY

- Open the width of the gates, and keep the target closer to the center of the sheet.

Success Check

- Keep your head up and your eyes on the target rather than on the cups. Focus on where you want to slide rather than the path through which you are sliding.
- Keep your body square during your slide, with your stone positioned in front of you throughout the delivery.
- Slide as closely as possible through the center of the allowable opening.

Score Your Success

Score 1 point for each gate successfully navigated for a maximum of 16 points.

Your score ____

Shot Drill 7   Pop Goes the Weasel

Set up one set of stones, as shown in figure 5.5, with all the stones in contact with each other. You will attempt to deliver a stone that contacts the lead stone directly on the nose. The objective is to promote all eight of the original stones into the rings. Each shooter is removed after each shot is completed, but the original stones are not moved from where they end up as a result of the shot. This can result in some fairly complicated situations if your line is not precise.

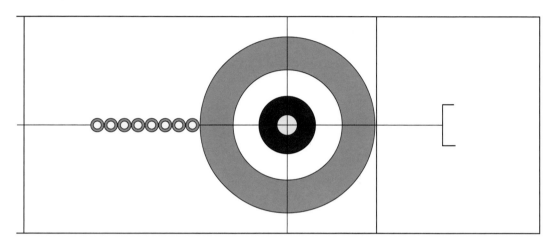

Figure 5.5   Stone setup for pop goes the weasel.

This can be played as a team drill, with each player throwing two stones each. The skip will call line, and the brushers will be involved to help manage the line.

TO INCREASE DIFFICULTY

- Do not remove shooters after each shot has been thrown. This makes the resulting situations much more complicated.

TO DECREASE DIFFICULTY

- Reset the original stones that did not make it into the rings after each shot.

Success Check

- Slide square to your target brush, and trust that it is in the right place to make the shot requested.
- Throw the appropriate weight because this affects the amount of curl on your shots.
- Make sure you have a clean release and the appropriate turn on your shot.

Score Your Success

Score 1 point for every stone that is in the rings once you have thrown all eight stones.

Your score ___

DRAWS AND HITS

Shots can be simplified into two categories based on their weight: draws and hits. Practically every shot that is thrown will belong to one of these two groups. A draw can be thought of as any shot that is intended to stop on its own in the playing area. That means it has the precise weight needed to come to rest in play without contacting another stone.

A hit, as the name suggests, is a shot that is intended to contact another stone and often remove the contacted stone from play. Hits require more weight than draws and are expected to have enough force that if they do not contact a stone in play, they will travel all the way through the playing area and out the back without stopping. That is the minimum force for hits, and as you will see, they may require considerably more weight than that. Hits are also commonly referred to as takeouts.

This is a very simplistic classification of curling shots, and in reality, the range of possible curling shots covers a wide spectrum of weights and purposes. There is always an appropriate weight for the desired result, and shots are not limited to any classifications we might use to define them. One fascinating aspect of curling is the way various shots can be used to accomplish different things. At the top levels of the game, players have the ability to throw a wide variety of accurate weights extremely precisely and therefore have many more options for accomplishing their goals. This flexibility is why you work on being proficient at a variety of weights and lines, so that you too can expand your options during the game.

Draws

Draw shots are intended to stop within the playing area, specifically within the rings. They are very much a touch shot in that very precise weight is needed. Draws are the quintessential team shot: In order to be successful, the thrower needs an accurate target to aim at as given by his skip; he needs accurate judgment from his brushers to massage and fine-tune the weight by brushing appropriately; and he needs the skill to deliver the stone with the right weight and line.

All players on a team need to be proficient at draw shots; they lie at the heart of the game. In any given game, getting a feel for draw weight early on is very important and needs to be communicated across the team effectively. By the time the skip throws his first shot, the rest of the team should have an idea of the ice conditions and how much weight is needed to get a stone down the ice and into the rings. The rest of the team needs to be able to communicate the weight information to the skip in an accurate and timely manner so the skip has some idea of the required weight for his shots. Weight conditions change during a game, and teams must monitor those changes as the game progresses so that players always accurately throw the correct draw weight.

The thrower is not alone with respect to weight control on shots, however, as appropriate brushing is critical on draw shots both for line and for weight. More will be explained about that in step 6, Reading the Ice.

Draw Drill 1   **Four in the Four**

The purpose of this drill is to develop the ability to consistently throw the same amount of draw weight. Your goal is to throw four consecutive shots into the 4-foot ring. Rocks are removed from the rings after they come to rest, and you will use all 16 rocks on a sheet.

To make this a team drill, the drill is run the same way except that players throw one rock in their normal rotation rather than two. The goal is to get the entire team working together to make four consecutive draws. In all variations, sweeping should be included.

TO INCREASE DIFFICULTY

- Count only the shots that stop on the button.

TO DECREASE DIFFICULTY

- Allow shots that stop inside the 8-foot circle.

Success Check

- Use enough weight to allow your sweepers to have an effect. This means throwing less rather than more weight.
- Ensure you throw down the correct line.

Score Your Success

Score 1 point for every stone that is part of a set of four draws that stop in the 4-foot circle. For instance, if you make four sets of four consecutive draws into the 4-foot circle, you get 16 points. If you make only one set of four draws into the 4-foot circle, you get 4 points.

Your score ___

GUARD

As the name suggests, the purpose of guards is to protect, specifically to protect situations that your team does not want disturbed. This may mean rocks in scoring position, or it may mean other guards. Guards are often placed in anticipation of setting up protected areas for use later on. They are also commonly placed in front of areas that teams do not want disturbed when, for instance, rocks are well positioned for their team. They function by blocking access, and they accomplish this by preventing subsequent stones from traveling down the path needed to affect the state of play at any given time.

Simply placing a guard in front of another stone does not protect the stone from being removed if there is sufficient curl to get around that guard. Ice conditions and the amount of curl on a sheet dictate how close or far away guards need to be in order to effectively protect various situations. The more curl on the sheet, the closer the guard needs to be to the situation to prevent another rock from affecting it. There is a point, however, where the guard can be too close. If a guard is too close to another stone, then the other team can propel the guard into the target stone instead of hitting the target stone directly with the shooter.

Guards are a subset of the draw family of shots because they are intended to come to rest in the playing area on their own. As with draws, the brushers play a critical role in placing guards because of how they can affect weight and line. The only real difference between draw shots and guards is their intended depth and purpose. Draws are intended to come to rest in the rings, while guards are intended to come to rest shorter and usually in front of the rings. Any rock in play that protects an area is referred to as a guard regardless of how that rock came to be in play. For example, if a takeout shot was thrown on a rock in play, and the shooter rolls to a position where it can protect part of the playing area, then the shooter will commonly be referred to as a guard even though it was not a guard shot.

Guards are often further classified by what portion of the sheet they protect. Guards that protect the center of the sheet, usually within 2 feet (0.6 m) on either side of the center line, are known as center guards. Guards farther from the center line are known as corner guards. The purpose of each is discussed more in step 8, Basic Strategy.

TAP-BACK

The tap is a shot that pushes a stone in play farther back into the playing area but not out of play. As play gets more and more complicated, teams will need to find ways to arrange stones to their advantage by moving them around the playing area. Angles between stones factor heavily in a tap shot. The final resting place of the shooter and target stone can leave them more exposed to your opponent rather than less exposed if the contact angles are not properly considered. The intention with a tap-back shot is often to get a stone farther back in a better position and covered when a draw cannot accomplish the same outcome. Taps are thrown with at least draw weight. The same weight on a draw and a tap will see the tapped stone stop shorter than the draw would have.

FREEZE

The freeze shot is another member of the draw family. It is extremely difficult to execute but is commonly attempted. A freeze is intended to stop exactly in front of another stone, ideally in contact with it. The goal of a freeze shot is to use a stone already in play as backing to make the first stone harder to remove. Freezes require very precise weight control, as often leaving any space between the shooter and the target stone means this shot has failed in its intention. There is little margin for error in a freeze: If your rock is thrown too lightly, then space is left between stones; if it is thrown too heavily, it bumps the target stone and also creates space. Line is also critical on freezes in order to create advantageous angles. If the stones are left at an angle that can be hit, both the shooter and the intended backing stone could possibly be removed.

If you can freeze your stone on top of another stone (figure 5.6), your stone is then much more difficult to remove because of the possibility that it will jam onto the backing stone during the takeout attempt. If you are able to freeze against a number of stones in play that are clustered together, then your rock becomes extremely difficult to remove.

Figure 5.6 Stone frozen on top of another stone.

Hits

The other major classification of shots is hits. In the broadest sense, hits are shots that intend to remove other stones from play. These shots obviously require more weight than draws or guards, and throwing the stone down the correct line is essential for success because the amount of curl decreases with the amount of weight on a given shot. Although the primary purpose of hits is to remove stones, an important secondary consideration is what happens to the shooter after contact. Hit shots are always called with this in mind.

A variety of weights can be used for hits, but it is a mistake to think that weight doesn't matter as long as it is enough. The skip will determine your target based on the amount of curl expected for your hit. Shots thrown with a lot of weight curl very little, while the maximum curl will be realized on a shot thrown with guard weight. As the player delivering the stone, you need to understand what is being asked before you throw and then throw the correct weight to accomplish the goal of the shot.

There are a number of common takeout-weight calls. Teams very commonly use the term *normal* to refer to the weight they have chosen as their standard takeout weight. Unless some attempt has been made by teams to standardize this weight call objectively, then simply calling for normal weight is meaningless because each player will have a different perception of what her normal is. One of the best ways to standardize your normal weight is to establish a hog-to-hog time. This means teams will decide how long the stone should take to travel between the hog lines for their normal takeout weight. Teams usually define normal take out weight as somewhere between 9.5 and 10.5 seconds for hog to hog times.

You also may be required to throw variations on normal takeout weights, both more and less. Takeout weight variations that are less than normal weight are classified by where your skip would want the rock to stop if there were no rocks in play. For example, *hack* weight refers to enough speed on the stone for it to stop at the far hack if it doesn't contact any other stones. *Bumper* or *board* weight refers to enough speed for the stone to come to rest at the back board if it doesn't contact any other stones.

Further up the spectrum, shots higher than normal weight are often simply referred to as *up normal* or something similar. Another specific type of takeout shot that requires more than normal takeout weight is the peel shot.

PEEL

The peel shot is intended to clear stones out of play. This means more than simply removing target stones. Peels are meant to clean up situations by both removing stones in play and rolling the shooter out after it has made contact. Accurately throwing peels is difficult because of the extreme weight required and because the line of the shot needs to be precise. The angle of contact between stones strongly affects the success of a peel shot. Some peels even run straight because of the speed and strength at which they are thrown.

NOSE HIT

A nose hit is a shot that is intended to contact a stone in play as fully as possible such that the shooter does not move after contact. This is a common version of the takeout shot. The location of the shooter after removing a stone is a tactical decision that teams need to consider when calling a shot. An example of when you may want a nose hit would be on the final shot of an end if your opponent is sitting one stone on the button. Hitting that stone and staying right there will give you a point . An example of when a nose hit is not ideal is when removing a guard. If you simply hit the guard and stay there, your rock essentially serves as the guard it just removed.

HIT AND ROLL

Sometimes hit-weight shots are used to roll the shooter or to have it hit another stone at an angle and then slide to a position that was not accessible with a lower-weight shot. This type of shot is simply called a *hit and roll*. It is usually first and foremost a hit with the added benefit of rolling the shooter into a position of increased value for your team. This is not always the case. In some instances, the primary purpose of a hit and roll is to get your team's stone into an advantageous position. If, however, you can throw a draw shot to get a stone into position, that is preferred over a hit and roll if you don't need to make the hit.

Sometimes a hit and roll will be referred to as an *in/off*. An in/off is really just a hit and roll where the shooter goes *in* to a particular position by hitting and rolling *off* a stationary stone.

DOUBLE TAKEOUT

The double takeout is nothing more than a takeout intended to remove two stones from play in a single shot. The shooter hits the first stone and then rolls in the direction of the second stone. Doubles require a good knowledge of how rocks respond to each other after making contact. The contact angle is critical on the initial hit to ensure that the rolling shooter contacts the second stone in the right place. The shooter also must have sufficient energy to remove both stones from play. Sometimes, the shooter is intended to go out of play as well, but not always. As your skill in shot making progresses, you might run into situations where more than two stones need to be removed with a single shot. This is a rare occurrence and should not be attempted if you have not developed the skill set to accomplish such shots.

RUN-BACK

A run-back is a shot that uses a stone already in play to hit another one in play. One stone closer to the hog line is hit and run back into another stone to remove that second stone. This is similar to a tap-back, but a run-back requires more weight because it needs to move two stones with enough force to remove the second stone contacted. Again, both weight and line are critical for success, and understanding angles and how curling stones behave is extremely important for skips calling this type of shot.

TICK

The tick shot is a very specific shot used to move (but not remove) a stone that is protected by the free guard zone rule, which states that you cannot remove an opponent's rock in the free guard zone until the fifth rock of the end. The free guard zone is therefore an area of protection for guards for a limited amount of time at the beginning of the end. The rule does allow for stones to be moved around within the playing area during this brief time of protection, however, and that is where the tick comes into play. The tick shot is an attempt to move rocks into a more favorable position without removing them from play. Usually hack weight or a similar weight will be thrown on a shot with the intention of contacting a guard and pushing it to a new position, either off to the side or into the rings. These shots are thrown only by leads since the free guard zone rule applies only to the first four shots in a given end. Doing this accurately and effectively is considered to be one of the most difficult shots in curling. The final resting position of the shooter is important, as you will see when we discuss strategy.

THROW-THROUGH

Believe it or not, on occasion the skip will call you to simply throw a stone away. The reasons for this peculiar request will become clearer during the discussion on strategy. A throw-through is as simple as it sounds. You still need to slide properly and adhere to all the delivery rules, but your intention is to simply deliver a stone without affecting the playing area. You know that the ice conditions change with respect to weight and line as the game progresses, and the throw-through can be used to gain important information about ice conditions such as how much curl there is in a particular spot. These shots are used sparingly and should be called with care, but they should give your team some information on a particular path or weight combination that you have not previously been able to discover.

Hit Drill 1   Hog to Hog

The purpose of this drill is to establish a benchmark time for your normal takeout weight. Have a partner with a stopwatch stand at the side of the sheet while you deliver a normal takeout shot. Your first target time is 10 seconds. Attempt to throw the stone so that it takes exactly 10 seconds to travel between the hog lines. Have your partner start the clock when your stone reaches the near hog line and stop the clock when the stone reaches the far hog line. Repeat this for 10 shots. Earn 1 point for a recorded time between 9.9 and 10.1 seconds. Any shot outside that time window is worth 0 points.

Next, declare your own normal interval time and throw 10 more shots, attempting to hit that window within 0.1 second. For example, if you declare 9.5 seconds as your target time, you must throw between 9.4 and 9.6 seconds to get a point.

The drill can be expanded for peel shots by changing the target interval time to 9 seconds.

TO DECREASE DIFFICULTY

- Allow for +/– 0.2 second on each shot.

Success Check

- Use your leg drive as your primary method of applying force to your shot. Resist the urge to push or pull back on the stone if you don't think your weight is correct.
- Maintain your delivery form, and ensure you have a clean release.

Score Your Success

Score 1 point for every time within your target time interval.

Your score ___

Hit Drill 2 Rock and Roll

Typically this is a team drill where the skip calls line and shots are thrown with two sweepers. Stones are set up as in figure 5.7, and each player throws four stones each. The goal is to hit the stone in the rings and to roll the shooter behind either set of guards. After each shot, the shooter is removed and the stones are reset according to the diagram.

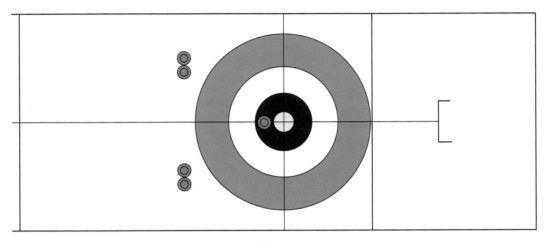

Figure 5.7 Stone setup for rock and roll drill.

To make this a team drill, the setup is the same except each player throws two stones in normal rotation. The lead throws the first two, second throws the second two, vice throws the third two, and skip throws the last two. Scoring is the same, but it is recorded as a team score with a maximum of 40 points.

Success Check

- Ensure you are focused on your target as you slide out. Keep your head up and eyes forward.
- Use enough leg drive to achieve the takeout weight required to make the shot.
- Slide straight toward the brush, and keep the rock in front of you during your delivery.

Score Your Success

For each hit, score your performance based on this scale:

5 points if the hit is made and the shooter rolls completely covered behind a pair of guards

3 points if the hit is made and the shooter is only partially covered behind a set of guards

1 point if the hit is made and the shooter is exposed

Your score ___

ANGLES

Step 6 discusses ice reading, and step 8 discusses basic strategy used in curling. By now, however, you can see that the game can get very complicated as the number of stones in play increases. Not every end results in multiple rocks in play, but there are times when situations get extremely complex. Skips spend considerable time trying to get their team's stones in a more advantageous position than their opponents' and to build on those situations as the ends progress. Often this requires accounting for how rocks are positioned relative to other rocks already in play. The angle between stones plays a significant factor, and so it is critical to understand how rocks behave when they contact each other.

For now, it is enough to know that every player needs to develop familiarity with how stones behave. Sometimes this is intuitive; other times it is not. When practicing, take some time to simply study how rocks react when they contact each other. As your skill progresses, this knowledge will expand and will become more and more important to you and your team's success.

SUCCESS SUMMARY

Curling has been called chess on ice with the major caveat that in chess, you are sure to get the move that you call out. Curling has the added complication of not always getting the result you call for. Successful teams can correctly and precisely execute shots over and over again. This sounds simplistic, but by now you know of the wide range of variations that could be called for any given shot, from the line to the weight required. Some shots are more commonly called in games than others, and of course it is the more common shots that you need to gain proficiency in first. From there your skills should expand so you are able to make more complicated shots. Your ability to control how much weight you throw and your ability to deliver down any line are the key factors in your skill progression.

It is impossible to predict from one game to another exactly what shots will be required, so it is critical to prepare for anything. The shots you have worked on here are not the only ones used in curling, but this step covers a broad range of commonly used game tactics. Gaining proficiency in them will give you an excellent skill range.

Each drill has been assigned a point value so you can evaluate your progress in shot making.

Shot Drills

1.	Progressive Slides	___ out of 12
2.	Interval Time	___ out of 12
3.	Climb the Ladder	___ out of 8
4.	Crazy Eights	___ out of 16
5.	Insane Eights	___ out of 16
6.	Cup Canyon	___ out of 16
7.	Pop Goes the Weasel	___ out of 8

Draw Drills

1.	Four in the Four	___ out of 16

Hit Drills

1.	Hog to Hog	___ out of 20
2.	Rock and Roll	___ out of 20
	Total	**___ out of 144**

A combined score of 115 or more indicates that you are prepared to move forward to meet the challenges in the next steps. A score between 94 and 114 means you can move to the next step with some additional practice. A score of less than 94 means you need to review, practice, and improve your performance in these skills before moving forward. Your development as a player will focus heavily on making shots, and so you should continue to strive for as high a score on these drills as possible regardless of what score you get initially. Shot making is the core of the game, and there is no ceiling or level beyond which you cannot improve.

Reading the Ice

As you developed your curling delivery, you focused on aligning yourself toward a specific target, even though that target was not the intended destination for the shot because of the curling stone's curved path. So the natural question is, where should the target be placed in order for you to make the shot you want? To correctly position the target, you and your team require knowledge of how much the stone is going to curl on any given path. Until you see stones sliding on the sheet, however, you have no way of knowing what degree of curl to expect. You must watch how the ice behaves and build a mental map of the sheet in order to correctly place the target. All players must develop ice reading skills, even though the final placement of the target is up to the skip.

A number of factors determine the amount of curl on any given shot. Some of these factors are out of your control, such as the ice surface and the stone's running surface. These are the playing conditions of the game; as in most sports, you cannot affect these conditions directly. However, the delivery also affects the curl within the parameters determined by the ice and stone conditions; that is something you *can* control.

Recall that ice preparation is discussed in detail back in The Sport of Curling. Keep that information in mind as you learn about how the rocks and the ice interact.

By way of review, let us examine what happens to a curling rock as it travels down a sheet of ice. Stones are delivered with a rotation on them and will take a curved path, the arc of which will be in the direction of the applied rotation. This is true for every shot on every sheet of curling ice. The degree to which the stone curls varies from facility to facility, from sheet to sheet, and often from one path on a sheet to another path on the same sheet. However, the amount of curl is not determined only by the playing conditions.

WEIGHT CONSIDERATIONS

The amount of curl directly depends on the amount of weight on a shot. In general, shots with less weight curl more than shots with more weight. At the extreme, a shot with a lot of force on it may not curl at all, whereas a shot with draw weight in the same path may curl several feet. Reading the ice effectively means understanding how much curl a stone will have down a given path with a particular amount of weight. It also means understanding how the curl changes as the weight changes. As games proceed, players and particularly skips and vices will build virtual maps of ice conditions in their minds so they will be able to properly position the initial target on every shot. The huge number of possible slide paths and weight variations is a vast amount of information to keep straight, and reading the ice requires good concentration, very good observational skills, a detailed memory, and a critical eye.

OBSERVATIONAL SKILLS AND CONCENTRATION

Every shot needs to be watched for what line it takes. Not every shot will be thrown down the line intended, and you'll need to register what actually happens rather than what was intended to happen. Each shot must be watched in its entirety so you see the full nature of the curl. If you neglect to watch a shot to completion, you run the risk of missing any potential finish the rock may have. Finish is the final bit of curl, often a significant amount of movement that can be used later to help hide rocks behind others. Concentrating on the curl, shot after shot, requires focus and more than a little discipline.

MISSTEP
You don't watch the entire shot from the slide to the point where the rock comes to rest.

CORRECTION
Develop the habit of mentally recording each shot. Mentally link the slide path to a final result to help complete the mind map of the sheet.

Again, primarily the skip will be watching for the finish, but all players should watch as many shots as possible to build a bank of information for their sheet. If all the players on a team are watching shots and building their own store of information, then it relieves some of the pressure on the skip if she is struggling with where to place the brush. It also helps you visualize a shot before you throw it if you know the path your shot is intended to take. Watching each shot also keeps all players engaged in the game. Because curling is a turn-based sport, there are times when your team will be simply waiting for the other team to complete their turn. Getting into position to watch shots keeps your mind on the game when it is not your team's turn to throw.

POSITIONING

The best perspective when watching the curl on a shot is in line with that shot, either with it coming toward you (figure 6.1a) or with it moving away from you (figure 6.1b)

As a brusher, it can be fairly difficult to watch the line on your own team's shots because of your position. You cannot get in behind the rock as it travels down the sheet because you need to be in a position beside the stone to brush it. As a thrower, you need to watch your own shots to see how they behave; you are in a good position behind the stone to do this, but you will need to exercise some caution and be critical of what you are observing. Remember, the stone is going to curl away from the line

Figure 6.1 Watching the curl of a shot: (*a*) shot coming toward you; (*b*) shot moving away from you.

down which you just slid. At some point during your shot, you won't be behind the shot as it travels down the sheet anymore because it will be arcing away from you. As long as you're aware of this perspective, you can still gain important knowledge on how the ice and stones are behaving.

When the opposition is delivering, there are particular positions you must be in depending on who will be throwing next. If it is your turn to deliver, then you should be getting ready to throw as soon as the opposing player has left the hack on his delivery. This makes it difficult to watch the shot, and you should not delay your preparation to do so. If you are the skip at the far end, you are in an ideal position to watch your opponent's stone. If you are about to brush your team's shot, you must be positioned at the side line, ideally at the hog line closest to the throwing end while your opponent is in motion. Once the opposing player's stone has crossed the throwing-end hog line, you may get behind your opponent to watch the shot as it travels down the ice, and you should get into the habit of doing so. In all cases, when you are watching shots, you should try to watch the entire path of the stone. Don't assume you know what is going to happen at the end of a shot—as already noted, ice conditions change throughout the game and knowing the finish of shots is a critical part of ice reading.

MISSTEP

You don't watch the curl on your opponents' shots.

CORRECTION

Develop a routine for between shots that you follow. Establish where you need to stand to get into position to clearly see your opponents' shots as they travel down the sheet.

Some paths are more commonly used than others. When similar paths are used repeatedly, it is easier to keep track of that part of the sheet. Other paths are used more rarely, and these can be more challenging to get a read on. Because of the nature of the game, you never know when you will need to use these less common paths, so it is very important to know as much about your sheet as possible.

BEING CRITICAL

A critical eye is also extremely important when reading the ice. Weight and line have a great impact on the curl for any given shot; however, another major factor that affects the curl is the release and rotation applied to a stone. A player may slide down a particular line, for instance, but give the stone a slight sideways push upon release that propels it down a different line than intended. This type of motion is often referred to as *setting the stone*. Players can set the stone out, meaning away from the body during the release (figure 6.2*a*), or they can set the stone in, meaning closer to the body (figure 6.2*b*). This is often related to which handle has been thrown on the stone. Setting a stone puts it on a different path than the one you are sliding down, and if you do not realize you have done it, it can give you a false impression about what is happening on the ice. At the top levels, players will practice purposely setting the stone in order to get different effects or amounts of curl. This is a very-high level skill that should not be considered at the beginner level. Players watching the shot need to observe the release to make sure nothing from the release affected the line.

Another factor in the release that can affect the curl is the amount of rotation on the stone. Stones with little rotation will curl more than stones with more rotation. If a shot has less than the desired rotation on it, there will be an exaggerated curl. If a shot has more than the desired rotation, then it will have less curl than expected. If you do not observe this portion of the delivery, then you may get a false impression

Figure 6.2 Setting the stone in the delivery: (*a*) setting the stone out; (*b*) setting the stone in.

of the actual amount of curl. It may sound tempting to try to manipulate the amount of curl by changing the amount of rotation you put on the stone. In theory, this can be done, and at the highest levels it occasionally is, often to try to get curl on ice that is otherwise very straight. Again, this requires an extremely high skill level and should not be attempted by beginners. Instead, you should strive for consistency.

On most ice surfaces, rotations of more or less than 2 1/2 to 3 1/2 rotations will give you unpredictable curl. This is the reason we strive to hit that sweet spot of rotation on our shots—that amount of rotation yields the most consistent curl.

As a thrower, you need to be honest with yourself and critical of your performance so you can give the rest of the team an accurate impression of how well you threw your shot. If you know, for instance, that you shoved a rock off the line but no one else on your team detected it, you need to relay that information as soon as possible to your brushers, then let your skip know so she can factor that information into the result observed on your shot.

The impact of the release is one reason that players should be critical of the information they observe when watching their opposition throw. It can be misleading to watch your opponents throw if you are not familiar with their releases. Teams will be quite familiar with their own releases and so will be used to the idiosyncrasies in curl that result from their deliveries. Unless you have a critical eye, you may miss these small movements that have a big impact.

MISSTEP

You don't observe the release when watching a shot.

CORRECTION

Establish a habit of specifically watching as the rock leaves the player's hand and then counting the rock's rotations. Also get into the habit of standing in line with the shot as you watch it rather than to the side. Both will give you clues about how clean the release was.

BREAK POINT

Another factor that players need to understand is the nature of the path the stone takes. You know the path is a curve, but the exact nature of that arc is not always the same. Sometimes a stone will begin to curl immediately upon release, but most commonly, the stone will travel in a straight line extending from the slide path for a certain distance, then break into a curve. It is very important to understand where this break point is.

The impact of brushers needs to be considered in order to accurately read the ice. Brushing reduces the amount of curl on a given shot, although how much depends heavily on how good the brushers are. However, the straightening effect that brushers have on a shot is usually higher before the break point. Once the stone begins to curl significantly, it is harder to reduce the curl with brushing.

Again, this is another factor that can be influenced by the release. If one stone is released much earlier than another, the break point will come earlier. For this reason, teams often work to develop a common release point to reduce the factors that skips need to keep in mind when calling ice for shots. Figure 6.3 demonstrates how a different release point will have a different result even with the same initial target.

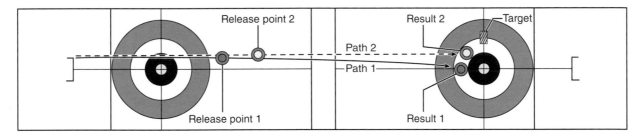

Figure 6.3 Break point and the effect of release.

ICE CONSIDERATIONS

Aside from the curl and curved path, another thing players need to watch for is flat spots. Curling pebble is very sensitive to heat, and it melts very easily if a knee or hand is left on the sheet for too long. These melted spots can drastically affect the path of a stone to the extent that they can ruin a shot completely by making it go in a random direction. Aside from avoiding creating these spots, players need to watch for any that have been created.

Curling ice is not a fixed surface, which complicates matters. Conditions at the beginning of the game will not be the same as conditions later in the game. Stones and players slide over the pebble and gradually wear it down. The extent to which it wears and the way it wears vary depending on many factors. You saw in step 5, Shots, that the delivery window at the near hog line is fairly narrow. This means that in every end, 16 stones travel over similar paths in the throwing end, and that translates into uneven wear across the sheet. Remember, this slide path becomes the core of the scoring area in the next end. Taking care of this section of ice and observing how it changes are very important. As the game goes on, individual paths become more unique depending on where the play has taken place, and that often means a reduction in the amount of curl. Typically, the edges of the sheet will run straighter than the middle later in the game. It is not uncommon for ice up the center within the rings to flatten because of wear (figure 6.4). This is sometimes referred to as fudging. Because they are not used as often, the edges can accumulate some frost buildup that slows the ice, meaning more force is required to get stones to the far end. It can also mean less curl on that part of the sheet.

Fresh pebble   Nipped pebble   Worn or flat pebble

Figure 6.4 Worn pebble.

The center of the sheet through the house will see the most wear (figure 6.5). Every single shot is delivered through this area, which means both rocks and players slide through here. The effect of that repeated wear depends heavily on how well players treat the ice and how the ice maker prepares the sheet. This wear and tear on the slide path is the main reason players should cool their sliders before taking practice slides at the beginning of the game. Considerable damage can be done to this part of the sheet before the game even begins if players slide down this path with warm sliders. In the extreme, this area can get flat, meaning the pebble mostly wears away to nothing. Stones will lose their speed very quickly on flat ice because there is simply too much friction without the pebble for stones to keep their momentum. Once ice becomes flat, there is nothing that can be done to rejuvenate the surface during a game. Recognizing the conditions is very important so that appropriate weight calls can be made.

Flat ice does not happen just in the rings. Flat spots or paths can develop anywhere on the sheet and can make playing the game extremely difficult. Teams can

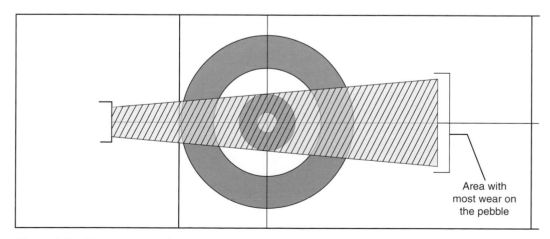

Area with most wear on the pebble

Figure 6.5 The center of the sheet through the house is where the pebble will wear the most.

either avoid these areas by directing play to a different part of the sheet or just try to manage how the shots travel through these areas.

Thankfully, flat ice is fairly rare. Ice making has risen to a level where ice makers can create more robust pebble that does not break down as quickly. Still, it is important for teams to be on the lookout for this effect and vigilant about how they treat the playing surface. Often, when players think a rock has picked, or caught debris under it, it has actually run through a flat spot. Generally, flat spots are caused by inconsiderate players who leave a hand or knee on the ice for too long after delivering a shot. The heat from their bodies quickly melts the pebble in a local area and creates a flat spot. This does not benefit either team in any way.

MISSTEP

You create flat spots during your delivery by resting a body part on the ice after your release.

CORRECTION

Establish a habit of standing up to observe your shot once your delivery has been completed. Alternatively, crouch behind the stone on your feet.

MISSTEP

You wear the pebble down through the slide path at the beginning of the game.

CORRECTION

Cool your slider down before taking practice slides. This can be done by stepping on the ice and sliding down the side line to the far hog line and back before taking your practice slide. Also, take your practice slide toward the edge of the sheet rather than down the center line.

Another factor players need to be aware of is a change in speed of the ice. Pebble may be more rugged than in the past, but it will still break down during the game. This means the domed shape of the pebble will eventually flatten on top as rocks continue to pass over the surface. As that dome shape flattens, more friction will be experienced between the ice and the stones and the ice will start to get heavier, meaning more weight will be needed later in the game to get a stone down the sheet. The degree of this effect depends heavily on how the ice was prepared, the facility, and how the game has progressed. If a majority of shots have traveled down a common path, then that path will naturally wear more than other areas of the sheet. The curl may also straighten out over the course of the game. The degree of change on a sheet cannot be predicted and can range from little effect to complete breakdown of the ice surface, though this is a rare occurrence. Players need to be on the lookout for changes as games progress, otherwise they will not be able to properly place the target for their shots and will not be able to throw the correct weight.

Occasionally, poor conditions cause what is known as *negative ice*. This is also a fairly rare occurrence, but players should be aware of it. Normally rocks curl in the direction in which they are rotated, but there are times when ice conditions are so poor that the stone moves in a curved path opposite to its rotation This situation is also known as a fall in the ice. Typically this happens on the edge of the sheet. In these cases, the target brush is placed such that the rock will curl away from the direction in which it is rotated. Again, this is rare and is a result of ice conditions and not the release or turn. In general, on normal ice there is nothing a player can do to incur a negative ice condition through delivery. Some sweeping techniques can impart a fall on stones. A soft release or one with little rotation can make the rock act unpredictably, but negative ice is not a result of a soft release.

It is always useful for players to know how ice is prepared before their games. Ideally the pebble will be applied consistently down the sheet, followed by a consistent nipping or rocking. Nipping is done with a blade attached to a handle that lies across the sheet. The blade is pushed down the sheet with the intention of cutting the tops of the pebble off to level the running surface of the ice. Rocking does the same thing except stones are dragged over the sheet.

A sheet that has been nipped or rocked before game play will be faster to start than a sheet that has not been prepared this way. Also, if the person nipping or rocking the ice is not consistent, he may create lines or ridges on the sheet. Clues to these conditions can be discovered simply by watching the preparation of the ice. One example of a condition that can be created by inconsistent ice preparation is the formation of a ridge along the center line. Typically when rocking or nipping a sheet, ice technicians will run up one side of the sheet and down the other. If they do not overlap the center line, then that area will be missed and will have unflattened pebble all the way down the length of the sheet. The effect is that rocks will have difficulty curling over that ridge until the pebble there breaks down a little and will tend to run straight along the center line. Depending on the severity of the effect, rocks may simply take longer to cross the center line or they may not be able to curl over that line at all. This again is a fairly rare occurrence but is an example of how watching the preparation of the ice can give you insight into how rocks will behave on your sheet.

Ice Reading Drill 1   Line

One player throws four draw shots down the sheet before the drill starts. There is no way to gauge line without experiencing it for the first time, and so without some prior experience with the ice, any success initially with this drill would be purely by luck.

This drill requires two players: a thrower and a skip. The skip first creates a gate the width of a curling stone with a pair of pylons or other soft markers at some point at the top of the far house. The skip then calls the ice she believes will be required for the shot to pass through the gate with draw weight. This drill is intended to help you see the amount of curl rather than test your ability to hit a target. The thrower then delivers the stone at the skip's brush. The skip scores 1 point if the rock hits the pylon or goes through the gate and comes to rest in the rings. If the rock goes through the rings, regardless of whether it hits the pylon or not, no points are scored. This drill depends heavily on the partner's ability to throw draw weight, so points are scored only on shots that stay in play. This tests the skip's ability to gauge the amount of curl. Throw as many shots as it takes for 16 stones to remain in play, and score only those shots that remain in play.

Repeat the drill as often as possible with various gate locations across the width of the sheet.

TO INCREASE DIFFICULTY

- Instead of creating a gate, place a single marker that becomes the target to contact.

TO DECREASE DIFFICULTY

- Create a gate that is two rocks wide as a target.
- Place a gate partway down the sheet at least two rocks wide.

VARIATIONS

- Allow brushers on alternate shots. Try throwing one shot without brushers and then one with brushers to see how much of an effect they actually have down the same slide path. Recall that sweepers can reduce the amount of curl on a shot and can be used to manage the path of the shot.
- Alternate the handle between shots so that each shot curls to the target from a different direction.

Success Check

- Observe the amount of curl on each shot, and adjust the target brush to what you are observing.
- Accurately determine the cause of the curl, whether it is an imperfect throw or the result of ice conditions.

Score Your Success

Earn 1 point for each stone that hits a gate post or travels through the gate *and* remains in play.

Your score ___

Ice Reading Drill 2   Break Point

As with the line drill, one player throws four draw shots down the sheet before the drill begins.

The purpose of this drill is to learn to identify the break point in a curling stone's path. You will need two partners for this drill. Stand in the house and call a draw shot by placing the brush at some point along the tee line. Partner 1 throws a shot while partner 2 follows with a curling glove in his hand. Partner 1 delivers the stone and watches the shot in its entirety. Partner 2 walks beside the stone, watching you in the house. When you see the rock break, raise a hand or call to partner 2. When partner 2 gets your signal, he drops the glove to indicate the break point. Let the shot continue, and at its conclusion gather with both partners. If both partners agree that the break point was within a broom's length of the break point you identified, score 1 point. Perform the drill 16 times.

VARIATIONS

- Call the break point from the throwing position with the same scoring.
- The thrower and the person in the house both call break point, with partner 1 marking each identified point individually. If the two identified break points are within 2 feet (0.6 m) of each other, both the skip and thrower get a point.

Success Check

- Observe the entire shot from start to finish.
- Identify the point where the initial movement occurs and how much movement follows after that point.
- Identify the break point with different rotations on different paths.

Score Your Success

Earn 1 point each time you correctly identify the break point.

Your score ___

SUCCESS SUMMARY

Every curling surface you play on will be different, and this is one of the interesting challenges that curlers face. Once you have learned to consistently deliver a curling stone, reading the ice becomes critical. It won't matter if you can throw the perfect weight along a perfect line if you never know what line to take for a shot. Reading the ice is very much a mental exercise and is also very much a team responsibility. Primarily the skip will be the one spending the most time gauging the ice and how it behaves, but the rest of the team should also be observant so they are aware of the playing conditions they face. Learning to do this will benefit your own play because you will be better prepared to throw shots knowing how they should behave.

Each drill has been assigned a point value so you can evaluate your progress with reading the ice.

Ice Reading Drills

1.	Line	___ out of 16
2.	Break Point	___ out of 16
	Total	**___ out of 32**

A score of 25 or above suggests you have gained good proficiency at reading the ice surface in that particular session. Sharpening your observational skills is an ongoing process, and you should repeat the drills as often as possible on various ice conditions while tracking your progress. When you are able to score 25 or more on every attempt, then you have achieved a high level of proficiency.

Roles and Responsibilities

When you talk about positional play in sports, generally you think of where you stand on the playing field. In most sports, how you line up within the game is a huge part of how to excel. In curling, you do need to consider where you should be standing during game play and where to move as the play develops, but this is not the focus of the game. In curling, positional play is important from a slightly different point of view. Each player in her position has a specific set of responsibilities that define her role. How well a player accepts their specific positional role has a huge impact on how well the team will gel and ultimately perform. This step explains those roles and responsibilities within a curling team and helps you see the challenges in each while you find the one that most suits you.

CURLING TEAMS AND LEAGUES

Recall that a curling team consists of four players. The four positions are lead, second, vice skip, and skip, and they throw two stones each in that order while alternating throws with the opposition. As you will see, each position faces unique demands and has different responsibilities during a game. Everyone throws two stones per end, but only the lead, second, and vice brush shots. The skip is primarily responsible for deciding what shot the rest of the team will play. Teams up to a certain level do not have a dedicated spare player. In club play, when a team expects a player to miss a game, a spare will be found from the club roster. Only at higher levels of competition will teams have an alternate in reserve. Even then, alternates are usually not rotated into play midgame unless an injury or illness requires it.

It is most common for curling teams to form on their own as opposed to being chosen by a coach or organization. This is true even at very high levels of competition, although that does vary somewhat from country to country. At the social and club level, teams are almost always formed by the players themselves. Players entering the sport as adults are most commonly drawn to the game by friends and family, so their initial experience is usually a social one. It follows that newer players play with the friends or family that introduced them to the game until they expand their curling network and find other teams to play with.

Each curling club has a unique plan for introducing new players to the game both as individuals and as teams. Although there is no standard, there are a few common approaches that clubs use to help get players involved in the game. Usually it is up to the individual player to find and attend a curling club to learn what league best suits his experience and wants as a curler. To help garner attention for themselves, clubs will often have open houses where people are encouraged to come visit the club and get a feel for what it's like. Sometimes lessons will be given at the open house, other times it's just an off-ice introduction the club itself. Once you have joined a club, you'll need to figure out which playing option suits you best. Most clubs have a variety of social and competitive leagues, and it is common for clubs to have options for individual entry or team entry. Curling clubs recognize the need for players to come into the sport in a comfortable and simple way, and this is accomplished through leagues that are specifically designed to focus on the social element of the game rather than the competitive element. Social leagues have many variations, but lately there has been some success with open leagues that allow any combination of men, women, and youth to play together. This allows players to play with whomever they want, an attractive option for newer players who may be nervous about starting off with experienced strangers. Traditional leagues are typically organized into gender-based teams. It is common to have men's leagues, women's leagues, and mixed leagues, where teams consist of two men and two women.

Some clubs have novice leagues to help players get a feel for the game and league play. Novice leagues are run differently at different clubs, but the overall idea is the same: to provide an environment where new curlers can experience and learn the game surrounded by other new players. Players in these leagues are restricted in that they may have only a few years of experience. They are always free to join other leagues within the club, but this introduction gives them a basis to start from surrounded by people at a similar experience level. Instructors often work in these leagues to give players guidance.

Draw leagues are another common option. In a draw league, players sign up to play as individuals and the league organizer forms teams for a draw lasting for a certain time, say six weeks. At the end of the six weeks, the teams are completely reformed. This gives players the chance to get to know a broad range of people within the club.

TEAM DYNAMICS

One fascinating aspect of the sport of curling is the idea that it is a "little team" game. This little-team situation carries many implications that make curling significantly different from other sports. One example is how team dynamics play out within a little team. With only four players, personal interactions both positive and negative are amplified when compared with a larger team setting. Because of the nature of the game, each player on a curling team interacts with every other player during a game, which forces any personal issues to the forefront immediately. Conversely, the opportunity to bond with the team comes much faster and much more naturally in the small-team setting.

Aside from personality conflicts, a major source of tension and conflict within curling teams is a misunderstanding of a player's role within that team. To be clear, specific tasks as called out in the rules are required of each member on a curling team, both while the team is throwing and while the opposition is throwing. However, to achieve higher levels of performance, players must go beyond those minimum requirements. Often a team's cohesion depends on the fit of the four individuals and how they go about accomplishing these tasks. Each position on a curling team has specific requirements and demands beyond the rule book, and in order to succeed players must find the position that best aligns with their own personalities.

Players do not rotate positions during a game, and so to experience the requirements of each role you need to play a variety of games at different positions. The need for players to be suited for positions beyond simply having the necessary physical skills is common across many sports but is intensified within a little team. Elite curling teams consist of players who not only understand the requirements of their positions but also embrace those roles and work toward mastering the specific demands of each. Success for any curling team depends on this sort of dedication to fulfilling positional roles to the best of a player's ability.

Another very important aspect of the little-team environment is the effect each person has on the team as a whole. With only four players, the attitude and approach of each player has a substantial impact on the overall atmosphere within a team. The influence one player has on the entire team is much more quickly realized than, say, the attitude of a single player on a team of 21 hockey players. Everything regarding interpersonal interactions and teamwork is amplified in the little-team environment, making it essential for players, teams, and coaches to work on this aspect of the game and to fully map out the roles and responsibilities of each member.

One misconception about the game of curling is that experience determines position. To be sure, beginning curlers start off playing lead or second, but it does not take very long to gain the experience required to move. Players can move into vice and skip positions as soon as they are comfortable with the added demands of those roles.

Players who are not suited mentally or physically to one position need to find another in order to achieve the success they desire. Thankfully, even within a little team there is a place for practically any type of personality. The difficulty is sometimes finding the one best suited to an individual.

Once players have some experience on a team, the needs and demands of the positions soon become more apparent. At the very start of your curling journey, these specific demands are less of a priority than learning the techniques and game play, but they become more important as you progress in your curling career. Enjoying the game means in large part enjoying your position, and so it's important to understand what is required at each position as you progress with your other skills. Good team dynamics are essential for enjoying your curling experience and progressing with your skill development.

Some common characteristics are required at all positions. Certainly physical fitness factors into how much you will be able to progress in the sport. Fitness levels affect performance at all positions within a curling team. The specific movements required for a good curling delivery depend on muscle groups and combinations that are unique to curling. Curling is very much a game of control, so the ability to accurately throw a variety of weights is important for all players. Strength and stamina in combination with fine motor control factor into this heavily. Flexibility and balance are also important. Newer players should not be intimidated by fitness requirements, however. Getting started in curling is relatively easy for players of all body types and fitness levels. Fitness attained through other sports is certainly helpful, but to attain success at a high level, curling-specific training is critical.

It is uncommon for club-level teams to have a specific coach, although the club will usually employ instructors or other qualified coaches to help players with their development. Some clubs offer clinics throughout the season to help members improve their skills. Oddly, coaching in curling is relatively new, and only at a certain competitive level do coaches enter the scene at all. A unique aspect of curling is that competitive-level coaches are often chosen by the team rather than the other way around. Certainly, some teams such as university or college varsity teams are chosen by the coach, but most teams form on their own and then choose a coach to work with them. The addition of a coach to a little team can have a profound impact on overall team dynamics, so when teams do get to the point of choosing a dedicated coach, great care must be taken to find a coach whose personality fits that of the rest of the team.

Another aspect of curling that sets it apart from many sports is the strategy that goes into game play. Many critical decisions are made in a curling game, and it is essential that all players have a good understanding of strategy and the purpose of the shots they are being asked to play. It does not help team dynamics if a player doesn't know or care about what is happening during the game. Curling strategy is covered in more detail in step 8, Basic Strategy. To complicate matters, a huge part of success in curling is the ability of teams to accurately assess how to throw shots in a variety of changing conditions. This requires all players to observe game play and be good at communicating their observations to their teammates. Each shot delivered during a curling game is very much a team shot despite the first impression that it is all on the back of the player delivering the stone.

Although the fundamental skills required to throw curling stones are common across the team, many position-specific skills are needed in order for teams to be successful. What follows is an explanation of the specific demands that can be expected at various positions. Once you have some basic skills, you need to determine where you best fit with respect to these demands. What part of the game do you enjoy most? These descriptions can help you figure out where your favorite position might be.

FRONT END

The lead and second positions are known collectively as the front end (figure 7.1). In many ways, the front end can be thought of as a mini team within the team. The front-end players do the majority of the sweeping on the team and are responsible for brushing each other's shots as well as the vice's and skip's shots.

When people start curling, they typically play a front-end position. The major reason for this is to simplify their initial experience in the game. It is not a requirement for the front end to completely understand the strategy of the game at the beginner level, and so by starting in one of these positions, players can concentrate on developing their delivery and brushing skills without the complication of understanding strategy as well.

The front-end players share a considerable number of skill requirements, so it's worth discussing them together. The front end does the bulk of the brushing during an end, and effective brushing requires both stamina and strength. Brushing is discussed in more detail in step 1, Brushing, but it's important to note that strength for brushing is not limited to arm strength. Both core and leg strength factor in significantly. Brushers can expend considerable physical effort, and to be successful, teams need to be able to count on strong brushing late into the game. Within ends it can be common for the second to brush four consecutive shots and the lead to brush six consecutive shots. Players must be fit enough to ensure that the effort on that sixth

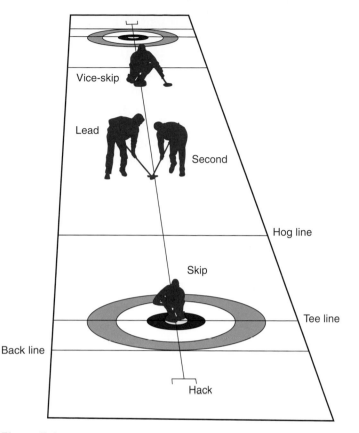

Figure 7.1   Player positions on the sheet.

shot is as strong as it was on the first, and they must also have the aerobic fitness to allow them to quickly come back to a relaxed state after this exertion so that they can throw their own shots well.

Aside from the physical demands of the position, leads and seconds must also be patient and eventually must understand game strategy, although this is not an initial requirement. Every shot thrown in curling is called out precisely by the skip of the team, and often the reasons for these decisions are complicated. Teams have a limited amount of time to play, so it is important for the lead and second to step back and let the skip make decisions on his own without having to discuss each shot. Strategic education for the front end can easily take place after the game. That being said, because of the little-team environment, the skip may want the rest of the team's input on particularly difficult shot calls, so the front end must be ready with information particular to the sheet of ice being played on. This means leads and seconds must be engaged in the game but also willing to take a secondary role in the decision-making process. How these conversations happen will be unique to each curling team. The level of conversation on shots will differ depending on the personalities of the four people who make up that team.

As mentioned, brushing stones is a critical job for the lead and second on a curling team. While brushing, front-end players must convey the weight of the shot to the skip or vice in the house calling the play so that she can make split-second decisions on how to manage the stone as it comes down the sheet. Clear, concise, and often loud communication with the player calling the shot is essential during brushing. Curling is often played in busy clubs or arenas where the noise of games from adjoining sheets and possibly crowds is present. Being able to project the appropriate volume on weight calls is an important requirement. In extreme circumstances, leads and seconds may need to resort to hand signals in order to get their information to the skip or vice skip.

Of course, in order to be effective, the information the front end conveys to the skip must also be accurate. For that reason, the ability to judge the weight thrown on shots is a critical skill for the front-end players in their roles as brushers. Both the lead and second must be very good at gauging when to brush stones and when not to brush stones. Overbrushing or brushing at the wrong time can be as detrimental to a shot as not brushing at all.

Lead

It is the lead's responsibility to deliver the first two stones for his team in any given end. After delivering those first two stones, the lead brushes the remaining shots as needed for the rest of the team. The lead will throw one stone, allow the opposition lead to throw one stone, and then throw his second stone. When the lead is between shots, he must be in a position that does not cause any distraction for the opposition. This is true for all members of the nonthrowing team, including the skip at the far end. This requirement is both specified in the rules and expected as part of the etiquette of the game.

Leads and sometimes seconds often have other duties as well when the opposition is throwing. Watching the opposition's stones to gain information on ice conditions is one such duty. Keeping the throwing paths clean by looking for and brushing away potential debris is another. Leads and sometimes seconds also generally get stones out for the skip before her shots. This little housekeeping duty helps teams play in an efficient and timely manner, and those small efforts can make a big difference toward keeping the game moving. The lead may be required to clear rocks off the rings at the conclusion of ends, but if the lead needs to throw the first stone of the next end, he will not do this. Instead, he will leave this task for his teammates and simply find his own stone and get ready to throw as quickly as possible.

The choice of shots required of leads is heavily influenced by the free guard zone (FGZ) rule. In the World Curling Federation rules of October 2015, Rule R6 (a) states, "A stone that comes to rest between the tee line and the hog line at the playing end, excluding the house, is deemed to be within an area designated as the FGZ (Free Guard Zone). Also, stones that are in play, on or before the hog line after striking stones in the FGZ, are deemed to be in the FGZ." Rule R6 (b) states, "If prior to the delivery of the fifth stone of an end, a delivered stone causes, either directly or indirectly, an opposition stone to be moved from the FGZ to an out-of-play position, then the delivered stone is removed from play, and any displaced stones are replaced, by the non-offending team, to their positions prior to the violation taking place."

Rule R6 was instituted in an attempt to get more stones in play. Prior to when this rule was in place, any stone could be removed by the opposition at any time. As players' skill increased and as ice conditions improved, game strategy turned to simply hitting everything out of play all the time and putting the very last rock of an end or even perhaps the game, into a scoring position. This was devastating to the sport; although that amount of repeated precision was impressive, it was fairly boring to watch and play, leading to a significant decrease in the popularity of the game. The inclusion of the rule has reversed much of that effect and now makes for some very interesting situations with many more rocks in play. More about how this rule affects the strategy employed is described in step 8, Basic Strategy.

The FGZ rule means a lead cannot remove an opponent's lead stones that come to rest within the zone. Since they are allowed to hit only in limited situations, leads more commonly throw lower-weight shots rather than takeouts and therefore focus their training on making draws and throwing guards as consistently as possible. This is not to say that leads never have to throw takeout shots or that they don't need to be proficient in making them.

How ends play out for teams depends a great deal on the lead's shots. Precise positioning of those first two stones can make or break an end. For this reason, leads need to have a very good feel for how much force, or weight, to apply to a shot so they can deliver stones a precise distance. This ability to throw with precision is known as finesse, or touch, in curling.

In reality, this is a skill that all players need, but for the lead, being able to deliver those delicate weight shots is essential. Teams cannot be successful without a consistent lead who can set up ends. A few factors complicate this, the biggest of which is the lead's responsibility for sweeping. The lead is one of the two brushers for the skip's shots, which are usually very critical and often require intense brushing. As a result, the lead commonly has to throw the first shot of an end less than a minute after brushing a big shot from the previous end.

Brushing requires significant cardiorespiratory stamina in order to be effective. Intense brushing can raise a player's heart rate significantly, and this can affect a player's ability to control her stone's weight when delivering. A lead therefore must have good cardiorespiratory fitness so she can appropriately recover in the short time span between brushing and delivering her own shots.

Leads must also be observant with respect to ice conditions and changes. Because they throw finesse shots primarily and because they are judging weight constantly throughout the end, leads must be able to accurately read ice conditions and clearly communicate them to the rest of the team. This skill comes into play both in terms of guiding the rest of the team and during brushing. The skip often needs to throw a finesse shot to score at the conclusion of an end. Information about the speed of the ice from the rest of the team, and in particular the lead, is essential so the skip can throw the appropriate weight on these critical shots.

Position Drill 1   En Guard

The objective of this drill is to gain proficiency in placing guard shots. Throw eight stones, attempting to place two stones in each of the zones shown in figure 7.2. Markers such as pylons can be used to identify the areas. Rocks are removed after each shot has been delivered.

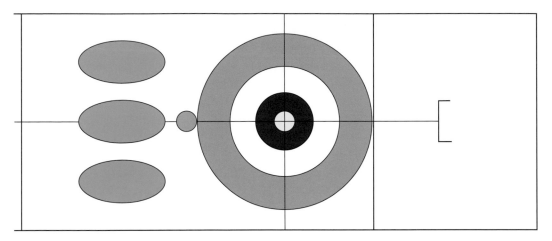

Figure 7.2   Target zones for en guard drill.

This drill can be performed as a team drill, with the skip calling line and brushers helping with weight. Each player should throw eight rocks so that the entire team has the opportunity to work on their weight control.

TO INCREASE DIFFICULTY

- Make the acceptable guard areas smaller. They can be made as small as desired and can even be shrunk to a specific point. To do this, place a pylon in the precise location where you want the guard to end up, and score 5 points if the shot stops in contact with the pylon, 3 points if the shot stops within 6 inches (15 cm) of the pylon, and 0 points if the shot stops farther than 6 inches from the pylon.

TO DECREASE DIFFICULTY

- Make the acceptable guard areas wider. That is, allow for shots to be less precise with respect to how far they travel. Scoring remains the same.

Success Check

- Think about the weight before you begin your delivery motion. Have a good idea of the amount of drive you will need out of the hack.
- Maintain your delivery form, particularly your release and turn. A clean release will ensure the most accurate result.

Score Your Success

Earn points depending on where your shot stops.

5 points: fully in target zone

3 points: mostly in target zone

0 points: not in target zone

Your score ___

Second

The player in the second position throws the second set of two stones for the team, again alternating with the opposing team. He is responsible for brushing the lead's stones as well as the stones for the vice and the skip. The second also clears stones at the conclusion of ends after the score has been determined. Like the lead, the second will watch the opponents' shots to help understand how the ice is running in various paths. He also needs to be vigilant between shots with respect to clearing debris on the ice.

The FGZ rule also factors into the typical shot requirements at the second position. As each player delivers, the game has the potential to become more complicated because of the possible number of stones in play. Teams often want to simplify situations by throwing takeout shots that remove stones. Because the FGZ rule prevents teams from removing the opponents' stones in that area until the seconds throw, the second is often called on to clear out those previously protected rocks. Therefore, he must be able to accurately throw these higher-weight shots repeatedly.

It is not as simple as thinking that a second needs to throw only takeouts, because teams do not always want to clear stones out of play. It is common for teams to want to take advantage of the stones in play as places to hide potential counting shots. This means seconds also need to be able to throw softer-weight shots if the situation requires it. This ability to adjust the weight between shots is a mental skill that factors into positional requirements more as the end progresses.

Brushing skills are as critical at the second position as they are at the lead position. Similar to leads, seconds must also get into a calm, relaxed state immediately after brushing stones. Strength and stamina are extremely important for both of the front-end players, as is the ability to accurately judge weight while sweeping.

Position Drill 2   One Then the Other

This drill helps you adjust your weight from light to heavy and then back again. Throw 10 rocks, the first a draw into the rings. The second shot will be a takeout of the first rock just played. Repeat this eight more times. Count 1 point for every successful shot. A draw is considered successful if it stops in the rings. A takeout is considered successful if the target stone is removed from play *and* the shooter remains in play.

TO INCREASE DIFFICULTY

- Require successful draw shots to stop in a particular ring. For example, count only shots that stop in the 8-foot.
- Require successful draw shots to be guards in front of the rings.
- Require that successful takeouts roll no more than 6 inches (15 cm) from the nose of the target stone after making contact.

TO DECREASE DIFFICULTY

- Allow any draw shot that is in play to count as successful whether it's a guard or in the rings.
- Allow any takeout that removes the target stone to count as successful whether it remains in play or not.

VARIATION

Often, seconds will be asked to throw peel shots on guards, so one variation of this drill is to throw a guard with a first shot then a peel with the second. One point for a guard if it stops in front of the rings and one point for the peel if it removes the target stone and rolls out of play itself.

Success Check

- Draws thrown after the takeouts are not too heavy and are staying in play.
- Hits have proper takeout weight and enough force to remove target stones.
- Each shot starts with a proper approach, and you mentally check that you understand the weight you need to throw.

Score Your Success

Score 1 point for every successful draw and 1 point for every successful takeout.

Your score ___

Position Drill 3   Keepaway

This drill improves a number of skills at once. It requires a partner and can also be played as a one-on-one game. Your partner will deliver a stone with the intention of having it stop in the rings. You, as the brusher, must prevent that either by over-brushing the shot if it is heavy or leaving it short if it does not have enough weight. This helps you develop weight judgment as a sweeper. It also helps you develop stamina, as some shots will be swept hard end to end. Your partner should throw 16 rocks, with each shot worth 1 point. Every rock that does *not* stop in the rings is worth 1 point.

In the one-on-one version, each player takes turns throwing stones. The goal is the same, to get your stones in the rings when you are throwing and to use accurate judgment to prevent shots from stopping in the rings when you are brushing. The successful player gets the point on each shot. Sixteen rocks are thrown (eight by each player), with each shot worth 1 point.

Success Check

- Gauge the weight on the rock early during the shot. An early jump on a slightly heavy stone can make the difference.
- Constantly review your estimate of the weight while it travels down the sheet.
- Be ready to brush the stone at all times during the shot.

Score Your Success

For the partner version, score 1 point for every rock that does not stop in the rings. For the one-on-one version, score 1 point each time you are successful in your goal.

Your score ___

BACK END

Similar to the way the lead and second are known as the front end, the skip and vice are collectively known as the back end on a curling team. The vice and skip can be thought of as the second mini team within the greater team. This pairing shares many skill requirements that are not as critical for the front-end players.

Both players need to have an intimate knowledge of curling strategy as well as good ice reading abilities. The skip is responsible for calling out all the team's shots throughout the game and often relies heavily on the input of the vice skip, particularly when calling his own shots. Another responsibility of this pairing is to call for brushing during shots, and it takes good observational skills as well as good recall to do this effectively. To make brushing decisions, the skip and vice skip need to have foresight into how things might play out, and they need to analyze many aspects of the shot in a split second. These added responsibilities of the back end are the main reason newer players do not start playing in these positions. Until players get comfortable with the physical demands of the sport, they generally do not get overly involved in this mental side of the game.

Skips and vice skips need to analyze a variety of factors in combination. Ice speed, line of delivery, stone rotation, amount of curl, and contact angles are just some of the things skips and vice skips need to consider during shots. Knowledge of all these factors is essential for making good decisions.

Just as it was with the front end, communication skills are important for the back-end players. Skips in particular must clearly and concisely communicate the shots they are calling. Often they must do this with gestures, as the noise level down the length of a curling sheet prevents verbal discussion. Again, because of time constraints within a game, skips have to make decisions on shots quickly and then effectively communicate those decisions to the rest of the team. Once the stone is in motion, they need to let the brushers know what is happening with respect to the line the stone is traveling on so the brushers can brush appropriately.

After the skip and vice skip make the shot call, they need to manage the shot as it travels toward its intended target. Their only way to control the shot once it has been released is through brushing, so making effective brushing decisions is critical. One way to think of this is that every curling shot is really two shots: The one you ask for and the one you get. Once a stone is delivered, skips and vices have to manage the shot they are getting. Ideally, the shot you're getting is very close to the one you want, but if it is off line considerably or thrown with drastically different weight than desired, skips must consider a plan B and manage brushing of the shot appropriately. This must be done very quickly in order to salvage something good out of a potential miss and sometimes there is no saving a poorly thrown rock. Still, the player in the house has to have a good understanding of what is happening and what the potential outcomes are so that quick decisions can be made.

Vice Skip

The vice skip is the only member of the team who enjoys multiple names. Vice skips are also known as thirds or mates and are commonly just called the vice. The vice throws the third pair of stones for a team and brushes the stones thrown by the front-end players. The vice skip also takes over the brushing call duties for the skip in the house while the skip is throwing. To be clear, the skip will confer with the vice skip on the skip's shot call, but the skip will make the final decision on which shot is to be played, just as she did for the rest of the team. Once the skip goes down the sheet to throw, the vice skip is responsible for managing the incoming shot and for making the correct brushing decisions.

At the conclusion of an end, the vice skips from both teams are responsible for deciding what team has scored and how many points to award. This may seem odd compared with other sports, but a minimum number of officials police curling games and at the club level there are no officials. Even at the highest levels, if teams can sort out rule applications on their own without official intervention, they will be allowed to do so. Officials do not step in unless called in by teams or unless a specific situation requires them to do so. Occasionally, it will be too difficult to tell which team is closest to the center of the rings and therefore which team scores. In those instances, the vice skips use a specific measuring device to make the official determination. At the very highest levels of competition, an official will perform this measurement at the request of the vice skips if they cannot determine which team has scored. At all levels, all other players on both teams are required to stay well out of the scoring area while this is taking place. If any stones are moved out of play before both teams have agreed upon the score, the team that moved the stones gives up the potential points affected by the infraction. The vice skip for the team that scored is also required to mark the score on the scoreboard once a decision has been reached.

Aside from these tasks, vice skips have unique roles within the little team. They brush lead and second stones and then switch hats and take over for the skip during the skip's shots. Vice skips therefore interact intimately across the entire team more than any other player. They act as a bridge between the shot-calling skip and the primary brushing pair. Because of this, vice skips need to be good communicators, perhaps the best of the four on a team. They need to deliver information back and forth between the mini teams, because they are in the best position to do so.

Fitness is again important for vice skips since they do sweep stones as well. All the same requirements that the front end had with respect to fitness apply to the vice skip, although not as critically since the vice skip brushes fewer stones.

From a shot-making point of view, the vice skip needs to be able to accurately throw any shot in the book at almost any time. The shooting demands on this position are complex, and situations can be difficult at the stage in the game when the vice skip is throwing. The vice skip's shots need to set up the skip's shots, just as the previous shots have set up the end to this point.

Over the course of a curling game, skips and vice skips make a lot of decisions together. Their specific interactions and how they discuss shots are unique to the individuals involved. However, ultimately the skip needs to make the call. This puts the vice skip in the position of being a supporting player in that role. The vice skip needs to understand both the game and his skip in order to advise the skip of the best options. Sometimes the best decision is not the one the vice skip favors but the one the skip feels most comfortable with, and that can be a difficult situation for some people. Knowing when to push for one option that the skip may not like and when to defer to the skip's own preferences can be a difficult line to tread. Ultimately, it means the vice skip needs to be able to put his ego in check and always make sure he is acting in the best interests of the team during the decision-making process.

The broad range of skills and responsibilities of the vice skip requires a person who is versatile in many different aspects of the game, from attitude and physical ability to shot-making skills. Players who are not well versed across these skill sets will not succeed at or enjoy the vice skip position.

Position Drill 4   Scoring

Six scoring situations are illustrated in figures 7.3 through 7.8. For each shot, identify which rock scored and how many points that team scored in the end. Answers follow the scenarios.

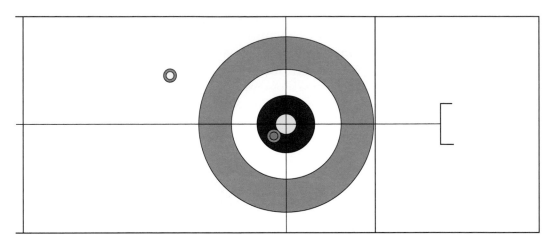

Figure 7.3   Situation 1.

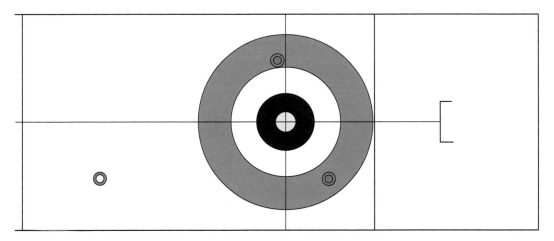

Figure 7.4   Situation 2.

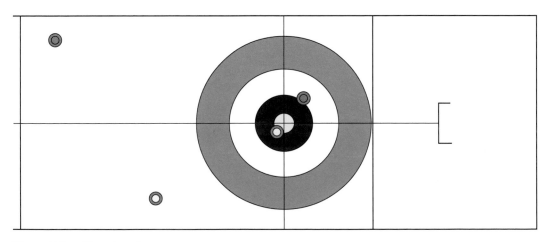

Figure 7.5   Situation 3.

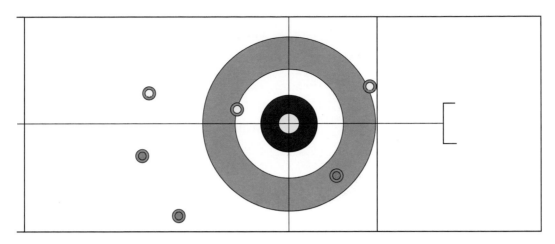

Figure 7.6 Situation 4.

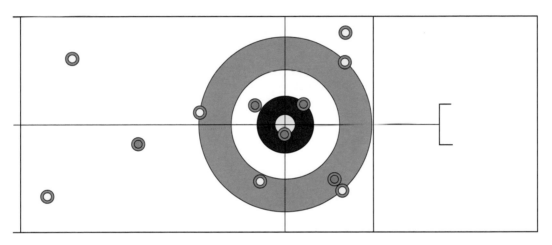

Figure 7.7 Situation 5.

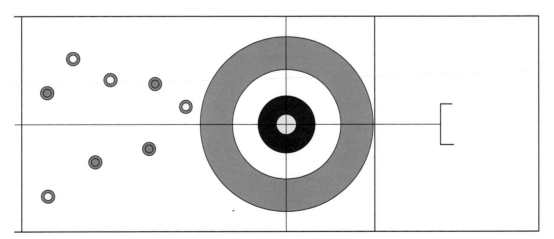

Figure 7.8 Situation 6.

(continued)

Position Drill 4 *(continued)*

Success Check

- Play close attention to the rocks in the rings.
- Remember, only one team can score in an end.

Score Your Success

Check your answers, and award yourself 2 points for each correct answer.

Situation 1: Red scored 1 point. The single red rock is closest to the center of the rings and therefore is the counting rock. The yellow rock is not only farther from the center than the red rock but is also not on the rings and therefore cannot count in the scoring.

Situation 2: Red scores 2 points. Red has two rocks closer to the center of the rings than any yellow stone. Again, the yellow stone is outside the rings and cannot be counted regardless of how close to the center it is.

Situation 3: Yellow scores 1 point. The yellow stone is the closest to the rings. Only one team scores in any given end, and it is the team whose stone is closest to the center of the rings and on the rings.

Situation 4: Yellow scores 1 point. The yellow stone is closest, and although yellow does have two stones in the scoring area, the red stone in the rings outcounts the second, farther yellow stone and prevents yellow from getting more points.

Situation 5: Red scores 3 points. Red has three stones closer to the center of the rings than any yellow stones. The team closest to the center scores 1 point for every rock on the rings and closer to the center than the opponents' closest stone.

Situation 6: No team scores. No rocks are on the rings, and therefore no rocks are eligible to be counted.

Your score ___

Skip

Skips throw the final pair of stones for their team during a curling end. Skips do not brush shots and are required to do only minimal sweeping within the house. Skips are allowed to brush their own stones inside the hog line and are also allowed to brush opponent's stones after the opponent's stones have reached the tee line at the scoring end of the sheet. The shots a team throws are all called out by the skip throughout the game. After throwing their last rock, skips are at the opposite end to the scoring area and so do not generally help clear rocks when ends are complete, nor do they participate in the decision on which team scored.

Curling teams don't have captains that fit the common definition of the role, but the skip position is as close as it gets. Typically a captain on a team is identified as the leader, often the best player on the team. The role of captain often encompasses a leadership position off the playing surface as well as during games, and this is where the distinction between skips and captains can deviate in curling.

The skip for a curling team does provide in-game leadership since one of her primary roles during game play is to call the shots the rest of the team will play. During the execution of the shots, the skip directs the sweepers. Skips often face difficult situations requiring precise shots, and so they must be one of the best overall throwers on the team. This aligns with our normal view of what qualities a team captain must possess. However, the little-team environment opens up the opportunity for other players on a team to have leadership roles. The skip role has some similarities to a baseball catcher. The catcher tends to direct his team on the field by directing shifts and by calling pitches. The skip also directs play for her team. The other similarity that both positions have is perspective on the playing field. In baseball, the catcher plays the entire game watching out toward the field and is the only player who does so. The rest of the team is looking in toward home plate during play. In curling, the skip's perspective is similar in that she watches the play coming toward her, while the rest of the team experiences the game as it moves toward the house.

Skip is the most mentally taxing position on the team, not only because the skip must be able to observe and accurately remember ice conditions but also because he must use that information to develop the plan for an end. Similar to chess, the skip must be constantly thinking ahead and mapping out various paths of shot progressions that align with the goals for a particular end. This mental effort often doesn't leave much for the other typical leadership duties that a normal captain might need to fulfill. Certainly the skip can serve as a team leader off ice, but it is not uncommon for team leaders to be someone other than the skip. Team leader is not an official role, but as in any sport, successful teams will all point to leaders on teams and curling is no different in that regard.

Skips must have a positive outlook and must be in control of their emotions. The mood of a skip has a significant impact on the rest of the team during a game and, if not managed, can impair the team. This is true for all players on a curling team, however, it is magnified in the skip position because of the responsibility they have for calling the shots. Successful skips are often calm and deliberate since a large part of their duties requires them to think through tense and difficult situations. Players who rush to judgment often don't make the best skips since they do not tend to fully consider options.

Skips do not sweep shots except for a very minimal amount within the house, and therefore the physical demands on a player in this position are much lower. That is not to say that fitness is not important for skips. The strategic planning and tactical decisions for a curling team rest on the shoulders of the skip with some input from the team. This requires a significant amount of concentration and the ability to think ahead while keeping in mind the knowledge of what has been observed up to this point. Skips must also know their team extremely well in order to gauge the shots they see and to respond to those shots during play. This mental effort is significant, and physical fitness has a huge impact on mental acuity. Some tournaments (*bonspiels*, in curling terms) require teams to play three games in a single day. That can mean more than seven hours of curling in one day, which can be extremely mentally draining on a skip. Not being physically fit can lead to a level of fatigue that impairs a skip's judgment and decision-making ability.

The amount of information a skip must manage can be overwhelming. Successful teams form game plans and have set plays for common situations, which can alleviate some of this information management. However, skips still need to integrate their knowledge of ice, rocks, and players into those plans. Knowledge of common curling strategy is essential, as is an understanding of the skip's own players' tendencies and abilities both as throwers and brushers.

A critical element that goes into tactical decision making is understanding how rocks interact with each other. That may sound simplistic at first, but how rocks interact at various angles factors heavily into shot calling. Curling stones all react generally the same way both in how they travel down the ice and how they react when they contact each other, but every set of stones is a little different. At the highest levels of the game, those small differences in rock tendencies can affect the level of precision players can achieve. That is just another consideration for skips, who often need to make split-second decisions based on some combination of all this knowledge. More detail about shots is discussed in Step 5, Shots.

Aside from fitness and a good knowledge of the game, players must also possess the right attitude in order to be successful as skips. Skips throw the final stones for their teams in an end, and because scoring takes place only after all the rocks from both teams have come to rest, skips have the last opportunity to affect the score. It is common for skips to have to make clutch shots to pull their teams out of a difficult situation. An axiom in curling is "if you can't draw, you can't skip." Skips often need to throw precise draw shots with very little margin of error under tense situations, and this requires a confident and resilient personality. Successful skips want to throw that last "brick" for the win. They thrive on that pressure and those situations.

Practically any shot may be required of the skip. Situations can be extremely complicated, requiring a high level of precision when the skip comes down to throw. Sometimes, by the time the skip is throwing, there will be little or no room for a clear draw into the rings, and so a precise hit or perhaps tap-back of rocks into the scoring area may be required. Other times, skips will need to make a difficult draw with a highly precise weight and line combination. Precision, a requirement for any position, is always a huge factor for skips.

Position Drill 5   Four in the Four

The purpose of this drill is to give you practice at throwing a precise shot under some pressure. The goal is to throw four rocks into the 4-foot circle, four times in a row. Sweeping is allowed if the team is available. If you do not throw four rocks into the 4-foot circle consecutively, the count starts over. Throw 16 rocks, and remove the stones from play after each shot.

TO INCREASE DIFFICULTY

- Require that the four shots stop on the button rather than just in the 4-foot circle.

TO DECREASE DIFFICULTY

- Allow scoring when you make three consecutive shots rather than four. Alternatively, allow yourself to score with consecutive shots that stop in the 8-foot circle rather than the 4-foot circle.

Success Check

- Focus on executing precise shots.
- Be confident.

Score Your Success

For every four shots that stop in the 4-foot circle consecutively, count 4 points. Maximum score is 16.

Your score ___

Position Drill 6 Taps

This drill is designed to help a skip with precision tap back shots. Set up five rocks approximately 1 foot in front of the rings as shown in the figure. Rocks should have about a 1 foot gap between them (figure 7.9). Throw five shots with the goal of promoting each of the stationary stones into the rings one at a time. You may use either handle. Score 1 point for each promoted rock that stops in the eight foot ring or closer. Promoted rocks that do not stop in the eight foot ring score a 0. Repeat the drill twice. This can be done individually or with the team so that brushing may be incorporated into the shots.

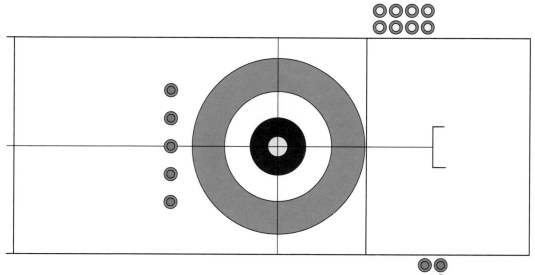

Figure 7.9 Taps drill.

TO INCREASE DIFFICULTY

- Move the rocks farther away from the rings. At the extreme, position them half way between the hog line and the front of the rings.

- Another increase in difficulty is to only score when the promoted rocks stop in the 4-foot ring. This will require not only good weight control but also will make the line requirement much more precise.

TO DECREASE DIFFICULTY

- Only use one rock and repeat the shot on that single rock five times. This will give you some repetitions on a single shot.

- Another decrease in difficulty is to score 1 point for any promoted rock that stops in the rings regardless of where it stops as long as it is in the rings.

Success Check

- Throw the appropriate weight for precise taps. This should be draw weight or slightly more.

- Assess the ice conditions with respect to curl and make sure you are taking enough ice to accomplish the shot.

Score Your Success

For every promoted rock that stops in the 8-foot circle score 1 point. Maximum score is 10.

Your score____

SUCCESS SUMMARY

To perform your best at any endeavor, you have to enjoy what you are doing. A curling team is a tight-knit group of four individuals working as a unit to consistently make intelligent choices and accurate shots. If you don't love the position you are playing, then you need to look at what other roles you might be better suited for. Curling provides a wide variety of sporting challenges, and there is a place for all types of personalities within the game. To a large extent, the front end of the team represents the physical force and the back end the mental force, although these roles are not really separated as simply as that. All players need some proficiency in all elements of the game, and it is the unique requirements at each position that make each role distinct. Part of your personal journey in curling is to discover the particular challenges that keep you motivated and engaged in the game. This step provides an overview of what is required at each position and also provides some drills and activities to help you get some practical experience common to those roles. Only through playing and extending your curling experience will you be able to fully discover the role that suits you best.

Each of the drills and activities has been scored to help you measure your progress.

Position Drills

1. En Guard   ___ out of 40
2. One Then the Other   ___ out of 16
3. Keepaway   ___ out of 16
4. Scoring   ___ out of 12
5. Four in the Four   ___ out of 16
6. Taps   ___ out of 10

Total   ___ **out of 110**

A combined score of 88 or more indicates that you are ready to move forward to meet the challenges of the next steps. A combined score between 71 and 87 means you can move to the next step with some additional practice. A score below 71 means you should review, practice, and improve your performance before moving on.

Basic Strategy

Dominance of the playing area can take many forms, from opening space up to allow for subsequent shots, to closing areas down through specific placement of stones. It can often mean setting up multiple options for access to different areas or closing off major paths while directing play to more difficult ones. Early in an end, shots are used to set up situations and arrangements that can be exploited later on. It quickly becomes apparent to a new curler that considerable maneuvering takes place to achieve desired outcomes and that much of this maneuvering is directed toward what will happen later on in the end. Sometimes shot calls early in an end are confusing for newer players because they do not yet have the experience to see ahead and anticipate how the end may play out. With more and more experience, you will begin to see the purpose of early setup shots and how they are used to achieve the goals of the end. Of course, you and your team are going to do your best to place rocks precisely where you want and need them; however, the opposition is going to be doing the very same thing. Also, as good as you are, not every rock you play during an end will stop in the precise location you desire. Simply planning for a shot in a strategic location is no guarantee that you will successfully get the rock in place.

Because of the many possible variations on every shot thrown, the combinations and permutations of rock positions are infinite. This means you have a great number of shot options every time you settle into the hack. No book could detail the number of possible scenarios and shot-calling options teams may face during a curling game, although patterns of common scenarios will emerge as your experience in the game grows. Deciding which shot to call can be a daunting task, but this aspect of curling is another of its major attractions. Many curlers enjoy the game primarily because of the mental challenge that exists in thinking through the various situations and combinations that arise during game play.

To be successful as a team, it is important to know which shot is the most appropriate for a given situation. This step provides a basic framework for making shot calls. It will lead you through a thinking process designed to make these decisions easier.

During game play, it is the skip's responsibility to choose which shot the team will play. The amount of team input on those decisions will vary from team to team, as some teams are more democratic than others. Regardless, teams have a limited amount of time to make shot calls, so even teams that like to discuss the options have some constraints on how long they take to do so. In fact, games are timed at higher levels of competition, so making quick decisions is important.

"Thinking time" is the current mode of game timing at most competitions where clocks are used. When curling games were first timed, teams were given a fixed amount of time to play. Similar to chess, each team had a clock that ran while they were shooting. The problem with this method of timing was that it penalized a team that played draw and guard shots. Draws and guards take longer to complete than takeout shots; if a team was playing draws more than their opponents, they had less time to make decisions. As we will see, when a team is down in the score, they will be more likely to play draws and guards and therefore this method of timing penalized them. To remedy this, the governing bodies adopted thinking time. Thinking time puts a limit on how long teams have to decide on their shots but does not put any restraints on the time to physically make the shot. During play, a team's clock will run while they are making the call. As soon as the called shot is delivered, all clocks stop. To be clear, a shot is delivered once it reaches the near hog line during a delivery. After that point, the shot is in play and cannot be taken back. Once the shot is complete and the opponents begin their deliberations, their clock begins counting down. This style of timing prevents teams from deliberating each shot for extended periods of time while allowing for the slower-traveling shots to be played without penalty.

Clocks are used only at higher levels of competition. At the club and beginner level, no game clocks are in play because of the need for a person and a clock to actually time the games. Recall that club play does not have officials involved, and the situation is similar for timers. Clubs often do put time limits on games, however. Typically 15 minutes is allotted for an end of curling, and many clubs have rules about what happens when you near the end of your allotted time. It is important for you and your team to make shot calls efficiently so you can finish your game in the time allocated regardless of what level you are playing.

Choosing which shot to play requires consideration of many factors. Wading through these factors can be complicated and settling on the right shot can be intimidating, particularly for newer players. Ice reading itself can be complex, and that is just one important factor to consider when calling your shot.

STRATEGY AND TACTICS

To get into the proper mind-set, let's make a distinction between strategy and tactics. *Strategy* is a plan. Your strategy is a guide to how you want to accomplish your desired outcomes. *Tactics* are the means by which you execute your plan. Tactics include anything your team physically does in order to make your plan work. Obviously this includes the shots you call, but it is not limited to that. Other systems your team employs during game play are also tactics. These systems may include communication methods or brushing techniques. Shot combinations that your team attempts to execute may also be considered tactics. The important thing to remember is that tactics are the methods by which you execute your plan and are not the plan itself.

Of course the goal for any game you play is to win, but the path from the beginning to the end of a game is never a straight line. Your opponents will be doing their best to make sure you encounter as many roadblocks as possible, so plans need to be fluid because you do not know what is going to happen as the game progresses.

Because the game is divided into ends, there are periodic breaks where game play starts over. Ends are a natural way to divide your game plan, and your strategy for the game will resemble an assembly of end plans. For this reason, we examine the development of strategy in terms of planning for an individual end.

As with any scoring game, there are really only three approaches or plans to implement. The choices are rather simple: Plan to score (offense), plan to prevent your opponents from scoring (defense), or bide your time (balance).

OFFENSE

Planning to score is considered an aggressive or offensive plan. The key to this plan is keeping rocks in play, so any tactics you use to keep rocks in play are considered offense.

Shots that keep rocks in play are typically softer- or lighter-weight shots. The most obvious of these shots is the draw. The intention of a draw shot is to have it come to rest in the playing area of its own accord. The stone is thrown with just enough weight to stop between the far hog line and far back line, although technically a draw shot is intended to stop in the scoring area (figure 8.1). A soft-weight shot intended to stop in front of the scoring area is a guard. Guards are used to block access to the scoring area and usually to block access to stones in play.

To score in curling, your rocks need to rest in the rings closer to the center than your opponents' rocks once all the shots have been thrown. Draw shots are a very good way to accomplish this. Draws require a good feel for weight and are very much a team shot in that the brushers can have a large impact on the outcome. *Finesse* is a word often used to describe draws and guards.

Any shot that keeps your stones in play or that gives you a potential scoring advantage can be considered an offensive shot. These may include freezes, in which the intention is to deliver a stone that stops in front of and in contact with one already in play. A freeze can be difficult to remove because of the backing of the other stone. Occasionally, higher-weight shots can be thrown for offensive purposes; however, this option is usually used when there is no possibility of throwing a softer-weight shot to accomplish the same thing.

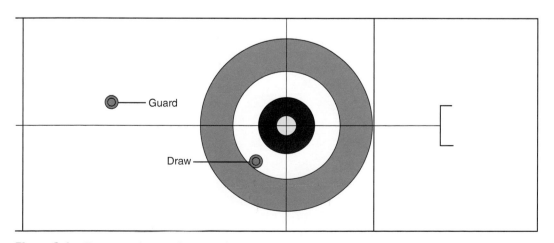

Figure 8.1 Draw and guard examples.

The free guard zone (FGZ) rule contributes heavily toward a team's ability to generate offense. Recall that the FGZ rule states that you may not remove an opponent's stone in the FGZ until the fifth stone of the end. This allows teams to place a free guard if they choose to. This obviously aids in getting rocks in play and therefore increases the ability of teams to generate offense.

Typically teams will choose to play offense when they have last rock. Because curling is a turn-based game, the team with last rock in an end has an advantage in that they have the last opportunity to affect the scoring area. With last rock, teams usually attempt to score 2 points or more.

Guard placement is an important consideration, particularly with respect to whether or not you have last rock. Because you typically want to try to get at least 2 points when your team has last rock, you generally want to keep a path open to the 4-foot ring. This is considered the most valuable part of the scoring area because the closer a rock is to the center of the rings, the harder it is to out-count it. Guards in front of the 4-foot ring prevent you from drawing into that area if you need to on your last rock, so you will typically throw guards to the sides or corners when playing offense with last rock. The idea is to attempt to hide a potential scoring rock behind one of these corner guards as the end plays out, then draw a stone into the open middle with your last rock and get your 2 points (figure 8.2). Your opponents will have something to say about your efforts so it is not as easy as it sounds, but that is the reason for playing corner guards when you have last rock.

If you choose to play offense without last rock, then you are at a disadvantage right out of the gate. Offense without last rock requires that you get a stone buried in the best position possible well before the last rock of the end such that your opponents are unable to remove it from play with their last rock. For this reason, center guards are used to generate offense when your team does not have last rock. Guarding the center establishes control over that area of the sheet closest to the middle of the rings. The other advantage of the center guard is that it can make the draw to the center difficult for your opponents on their last shot of the end. Because of the advantage the last rock provides, when a team without the hammer (or last rock) does score, it is referred to as a steal.

Teams will also play offense when the score dictates that they need to do so. Obviously if a team is losing in the final end of play, then they must play offense in order

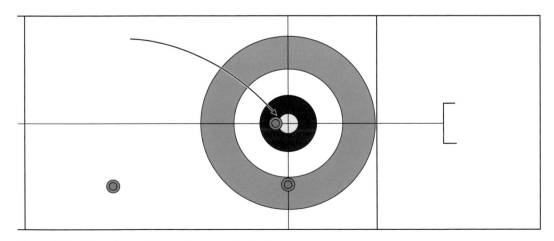

Figure 8.2 Drawing with a stone protected.

to win regardless of whether they have last rock or not. However, teams will play to the scoreboard earlier than that and attempt to gain an advantage in score well before the final end. Often, teams without last rock will work to force their opponents to take a single point in an end to give themselves last-rock advantage at strategic points in the game. This does not necessarily mean they will rush the offense or take risks when they are not called for, but consistently scoring with the hammer while limiting your opponents' scoring is a very successful approach. A curling game can be a back-and-forth affair, and if two teams are evenly matched with respect to skill, then taking chances by playing aggressively can backfire. With many stones in play, the opportunity to score increases not only for you but also for your opponents because of the possibility of guards, covering stones, and backing in the house. These factors make it difficult to remove counting stones and therefore increase the possibility of scoring for both teams.

Finally, teams may choose to play offense when they believe it is their strength. If a team is confident they can out maneuver their opponents with superior drawing skill, for instance, they may choose to play offense whether or not they have last rock and whether or not they need to score to gain a lead. Playing offense-first requires teams to be resilient and able to tolerate risk because of the potential for big ends to be scored against them. An offensive style has more risk associated with it, and teams must be able to rebound when things do not go their way.

DEFENSE

Defensive strategy is the opposite of offensive strategy. Where the intention of an offense-first approach is to keep stones in play, defense is about preventing scoring by keeping the playing area as devoid of stones as possible. Obviously, the primary type of shot used in this style of play is the takeout. Takeouts are intended to remove stones from play, generally opposition stones but occasionally your own if they are protecting the opponents' position in the scoring area.

The FGZ rule is designed to make defense more difficult. Opponents' stones in the FGZ cannot be removed until the fifth shot of an end, although they can be relocated within the playing area. Skilled teams use a tick shot to bump the protected guard out of its sheltered position. The tick shot is widely considered to be one of the most difficult in curling because of the extreme precision needed for both weight and line.

By the fifth rock of the end, the FGZ rule no longer applies, and teams playing defense will often try to remove guards outside the rings to minimize protection for potential counting stones. Just hitting a guard out of play is often not sufficient because if the thrown rock simply replaces the guard, then the protection still exists. In these cases, a peel shot or a hit and roll is usually called. A peel is intended to remove a stone in play and then roll out of play itself, removing any possibility for protection. Peels require an extreme amount of weight and very precise line and generally are not thrown by beginning players. A hit and roll (figure 8.3) can accomplish the same thing as a peel (figure 8.4). Generally, a hit and roll is thrown with less weight than a peel; There is a risk that the shooter will not roll far enough out of the way, potentially leaving it useful as a guard.

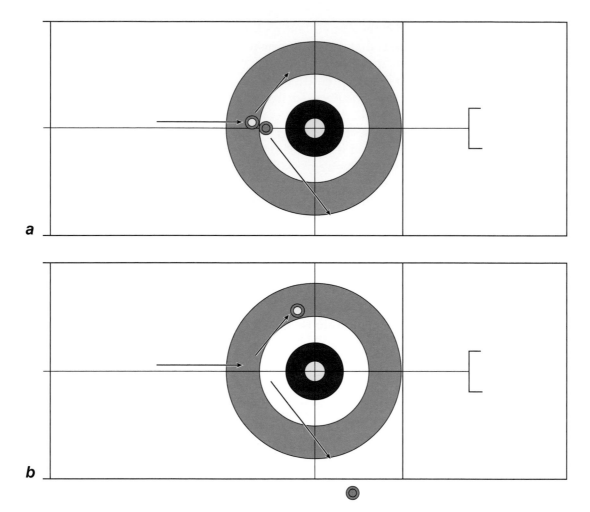

Figure 8.3 Hit and roll: (*a*) stone (yellow) contacts the guard (red) and (*b*) moves it out of the way, but the stone stays in play.

Defense is most often played when a team does not have last rock. When you don't have last rock, your goal is typically to force the other team to score a single point. The intention is to hold your opponents to 1 point and then score 2 or more when your team has last rock. The force is analogous to breaking serve in tennis, whereby the player who is not serving wins a game within a set.

You can also play defense when you have a definite advantage on the scoreboard. Because an offensive game leads to many rocks in play, your opponent could end up scoring when you intend to. Teams enjoying a sizable lead will generally switch to a defensive approach to reduce the risk of giving up points.

Occasionally teams will choose to play defense-first for the same reason that some teams choose to play offense-first, simply because it is their strength. This style can be mentally challenging, however, because the opportunities for scoring are limited.

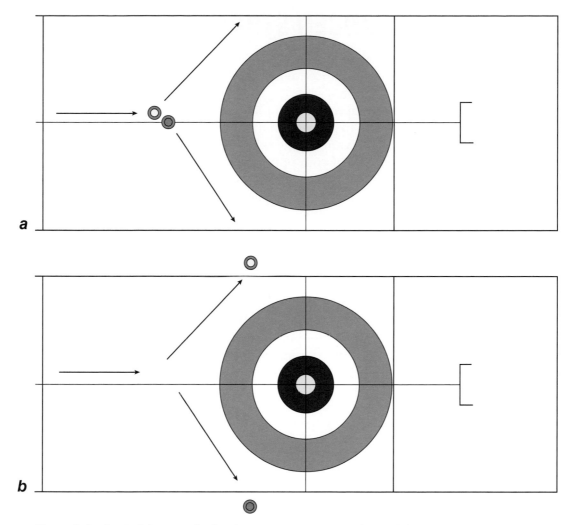
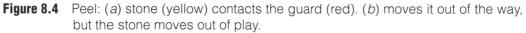

Figure 8.4 Peel: (*a*) stone (yellow) contacts the guard (red). (*b*) moves it out of the way, but the stone moves out of play.

Scoring becomes much more difficult when using this style predominantly, and so even the smallest opportunities must be taken advantage of to get points. Patience and stamina are important.

MISSTEP

You mistake a guard shot for a defensive-type shot.

CORRECTION

Guards are placed to protect scoring shots and are therefore aggressive or offensive-style shots.

BALANCED STRATEGY

A balanced strategy is aptly named because it is somewhere between offense and defense. Teams most often play balanced when the score is close, regardless of who has the last rock.

The purpose of a balanced approach is to play without taking many risks while keeping your options open. The first question that generally arises when discussing this approach is why would you want to play this way? Many factors can lead you to this style of play. If you are unsure of your opponents' skill level or the ice conditions, for instance, you may want to be cautious about how you set up your ends.

Balanced play is very much like "wait and see," with a significant caveat. This is not purely reactionary shot calling. Rather, it is more like setting up a situation with a particular goal in mind and then waiting to see how things play out. Balanced play cannot continue throughout an entire end, however. At some point you must decide whether to go after available points or to work to prevent the opposition from scoring. In other words, you have to eventually switch from balanced to offense or defense before the conclusion of the end.

Balanced play is difficult to manage for a number of reasons. First, you and your team need to be proficient at all shots—you will be required to play them all with this style. It also requires good team dynamics and good communication methods because once gears shift from balanced to the final direction, the team must understand that change immediately without a long conversation about it. Finally, determining the correct point to switch away from a balanced approach is difficult. Making that choice one shot too late or too early can ruin the end for you.

CHOOSING A STRATEGY

With an awareness of the plans available and how they are generally played, you are ready to decide which plan to use in any given end. A number of factors contribute to this decision, not least of which is your team's ability. Do not lose sight of the fact that the overall goal of the game is to win. When deciding which strategy to employ, you are simply discussing the path you prefer to use to achieve that ultimate goal. What should not be overlooked is the influence of personality on strategy. As you learn more and more about strategy in curling, you will discover there are usually many opinions about which shot is right in any given situation, and often the final decision will come down to personal preference between two viable options. This is not just a flip of the coin between two possible shots; rather, it is a choice that aligns with a player's or team's comfort zone or skill level. For example, there are times when clearing out the front of the playing area with a big-weight shot might be the very best thing to do, but if the players do not have the skill or experience to throw that shot, they likely will choose not to throw it. That doesn't make the shot selection wrong; it is simply a choice to align the skills of the team with the overall goals in the end.

Choosing which of the three approaches to employ in an upcoming end is relatively easy once you answer three questions. At first the answers to these questions might seem obvious, but you need to consider them carefully.

WHAT IS THE GOAL?

Do you want to score? Do you want to make sure your opponents don't score? Do you want to keep your opponents from scoring more than a certain number of points? An example is in the final end of a game where you do not have last rock. If you are winning by 3 points, then you want to limit your opponent to scoring no more than 2. That is your goal for the end because if you can accomplish this, you win the game. You do not need to score in order to win in this scenario, so attempting to steal the end is likely inviting more risk than is necessary and may put you in danger of giving up more than 2 points.

WHAT IS ACCEPTABLE?

What can you live with? In the previous example, it is likely acceptable to give up 3 points. That would result in a tie game, which possibly could be won in an extra end. Even if extra ends are not played at your particular competition, tying a game may be acceptable. It is certainly preferable to losing the game.

WHAT IS UNACCEPTABLE?

In this case, giving up 4 points is unacceptable.

You should see a pattern developing based on the answers to these questions. Determine whether you need to score, whether you need to prevent your opponents from scoring, or whether you simply need to keep the game close. The answer will lead you to a specific plan for the upcoming end, which in turn leads you to the most common shot selection for that plan.

In the previous example, it would seem clear that the primary goal is to prevent the opponents from scoring, and therefore you will want to play with a defensive strategy. Recall that defense means reducing the number of stones in play, both your opponents' and your own. It would make sense, then, on the first shot of the end, to either play a stone through the rings (throw it away completely) or simply draw it into the house where the opponents can remove it if they so desire. A rock placed in front of the rings would be protected by the free guard zone rule and would not help you in your efforts to keep minimal rocks in play throughout the end.

Strategy Drill 1   Identify the Strategy

Five scenarios are described (figures 8.5 through 8.9). In each case your team has just finished throwing and a description of the shot is provided. For each shot shown, identify whether the shot reflected an offensive, defensive, or balanced strategy. Assume that in each scenario your team is throwing the red stones and your opposition is throwing the yellow stones. Also note that in some situations there are no opposition (yellow) stones in play. Explanations follow the scenarios.

Situation 1

- End 1 of 8
- Red lead's first shot
- Red does not have last rock

- Shot called: center guard halfway between the house and the hog line. Was this shot offense, defense, or balanced?

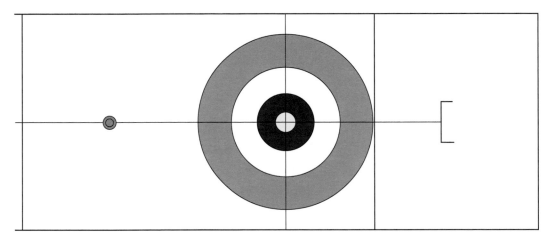

Figure 8.5   Situation 1: center guard halfway between house and hog line.

Situation 2

- End 1 of 8
- Red lead's first shot
- Red does not have last rock

- Shot called: draw shot to the top 4-foot circle in the rings. Was this shot offense, defense, or balanced?

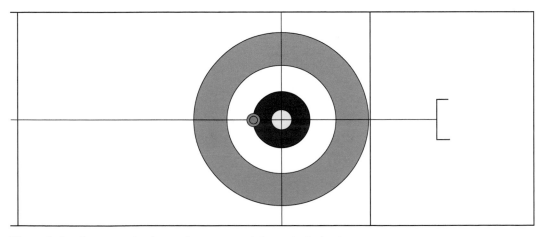

Figure 8.6   Situation 2: draw shot to top 4-foot circle in rings.

Situation 3

- End 3 of 8
- Red lead's second shot
- Red does not have last rock

- Red first threw a shot to the top of the 4-foot ring on the center line. Yellow responded by throwing a corner guard. Red's second shot was a draw behind the guard. Was this shot offense, defense, or balanced?

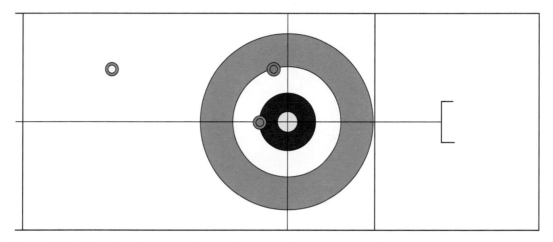

Figure 8.7 Situation 3: draw shot behind guard as the second shot.

Situation 4

- End 6 of 8
- Red lead's first shot
- Red has last rock

- Yellow threw the first rock of the end, a center guard. The red lead then drew around the center guard to the top of the 4-foot ring. Was this shot offense, defense, or balanced?

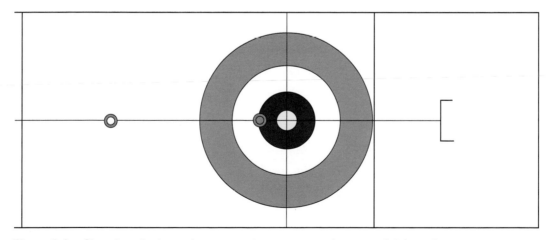

Figure 8.8 Situation 4: draw shot around center guard to top of 4-foot ring.

(continued)

Strategy Drill 1 *(continued)*

Situation 5

- End 3 of 8
- Red lead's first shot
- Red has last rock

- Yellow threw the first rock of the end, a draw to the top of the 4-foot ring. The red lead then threw a takeout to remove the yellow stone.

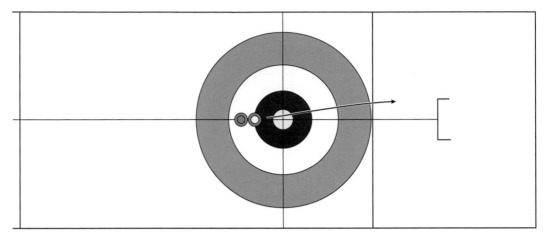

Figure 8.9   Situation 5: takeout to remove stone.

TO DECREASE DIFFICULTY

- Collaborate with other players, and decide the answers together.

Success Check

- Look for situations that lead toward more stones in play to find offense examples.

- Look for situations where there is less chance for either team to score to find defense examples.
- Look for situations that give the opponent a number of choices to find balanced options.

Score Your Success

Check your answers, and score 2 points for each answer you get correct.

Situation 1: **Offense.** The FGZ rule does not allow red's opposition to remove this stone. It is protected for the first shots of the end, and therefore this shot contributes to the number of stones in play. Regardless of what yellow chooses to do, this guard will be in play and available as cover when it is their turn to throw. It will be available as cover for subsequent rocks.

Situation 2: **Defense.** This rock may look like an aggressive shot but it has no protection whatsoever. It can be removed by the opposition immediately with no risk at all. It is the first rock of the end and there are 15 total shots to come, making it very unlikely that this rock will stay in its current location for very long. This shot is meant to entice the yellow team into hitting it and hopefully keep the number of total rocks in play to a minimum.

Situation 3: **Balanced.** By drawing behind the guard, red is leaving the shot rock exposed and available to be hit. By placing a rock behind the opposing guard, red has taken that same shot away from yellow and has made the yellow guard less useful to yellow. This is not an offensive shot because the potential scoring point is still exposed. It is also not defensive because it contributes to rocks in play. This shot attempts to put some pressure on yellow to decide whether they want to take risks by putting more rocks in play or to start cleaning out the house.

Situation 4: **Offense.** Drawing around the center guard is intended to place the stone where it is protected from being removed. The particular placement, top 4-foot, is a valuable scoring area, and red is attempting to get one of their stones into this region before yellow gets a chance to do the same thing. This is not a defensive shot because it is thrown into a position where it will be difficult to remove.

Situation 5: **Defense.** Removing stones from play reduces the chances that there will be much scoring. Even though the shot remains in play after removing the yellow rock, it is still not much of a threat to score because it is exposed and there are many rocks left to play in the end.

Your score ___

Strategy Drill 2   Pick a Strategy

In each of the following five situations, pick the most likely strategy (offense, defense, or balanced) that you would play going into the end. Begin by answering the three big questions:

1. What is the goal?
2. What is acceptable?
3. What is unacceptable?

Based on the answers to those questions, determine your plan. Explanations follow the scenarios.

Situation 1

Going into the eighth end of an eight-end game.

Score is tied.

You have last rock.

Situation 2

Going into the second end of an eight-end game.

You are winning by 2 points.

You do not have last rock.

Situation 3

Going into the fourth end of an eight-end game.

You are winning by 1 point.

You have last rock.

Situation 4

Going into the sixth end of an eight-end game.

You are winning by 4 points.

You do not have last rock.

Situation 5

Going into the third end of an eight-end game.

You are losing by 1 point.

You have last rock.

TO INCREASE DIFFICULTY

- Explain why you picked the strategy you chose. What factors specifically made the decision?

TO DECREASE DIFFICULTY

- Work through the examples with a partner or your team.

Success Check

- Recognize that situations in which you need to score demand an offensive approach.
- Recognize situations in which you do not need to score as defensive situations.
- Recognize that when the score is close and the game is not on the line, a balanced style can be used.

Score Your Success

Check your answers, and score 2 points for each situation in which you correctly identified the strategy to follow.

Situation 1: **Offense.** In this situation, you must score in order to win the game. You really have no choice. You also have last rock, and while you will generally play offense with last rock, the overriding elements are the facts that this is the last end and the score is tied. If you do not score, you will not win.

Situation 2: **Defense.** You do not have last rock, which makes scoring more difficult. Also, you are winning and do not need to risk the attempt to score. There is plenty of time left to build your lead as long as you do not let your opponents get too close at this point in the game. If you answered **balanced**, give yourself 1 point. Some teams and players may prefer to play an open style and push their opponents in this situation, particularly early in the game. Again, however, avoiding risk is key, so it would not be acceptable to pursue a steal and play aggressively. You risk giving up your advantage on the scoreboard and potentially momentum in the game.

Situation 3: **Balanced.** The score is close and it is the middle of the game. You have a slight advantage on the scoreboard and the advantage of last rock, so it might be tempting to play aggressively. However, there are risks involved. Playing cautiously here and scoring even a single point means you take a 2-point advantage into the next end. Playing with a lot of rocks in play to try to get 2 points may backfire on you and result in your giving up a steal. If you answered **offense**, score 1 point because the final decision between balanced and offense comes down to your personal risk tolerance.

Situation 4: **Defense.** Your team has control of the game despite not having last rock. You do not have to score any points in order to win the game; you need only keep your opponent from scoring more than 4 points in the remaining three ends. You should try to keep the house as clean as possible. Giving up a single point in this end is a very good result because that means you will go into the seventh and penultimate end up by 3 points with last-rock advantage.

Situation 5: **Offense.** The score is close and you have last rock in the middle of the game. You need to keep the score close and try to get your 2 points with last-rock advantage. There is no need to take extreme risks in this situation. Your goal for this end should be to get 2 points or possibly blank the end so you can try for a pair in the fourth end. Score 1 point for answering **balanced**. Keeping the score close is important at this stage of the game.

Your score ___

DEVELOPING AN END PLAN

No resource can outline every scenario you will face in a curling game. What you need in order to learn to call the game is a methodology that will help you quickly narrow the shot choices. This means having an end plan and developing the knowledge to execute that plan.

End plans are based on the knowledge of three specific factors:

1. The end you are playing in
2. The score differential at any given time
3. Whether you have last rock

These can be mapped out before a game, allowing you to prepare a strategy for varying situations. Some teams map out their preferred style of play and build a game plan based solely on these factors. Particularly at the higher levels of competition, teams will discuss strategy in detail before the game so they will be ready for certain scenarios when they arise. As you begin to call shots, you need to consider at least these three factors and have some inclination toward how you will handle them. Many teams take a few seconds between ends to decide how they plan to approach the upcoming ends, and often those discussions consist mainly of clarifying the answers to the three big questions covered earlier: what we want (the goal), what we can live with (acceptable), and what we need to avoid (unacceptable). Figure 8.10 shows a game plan mapped out as described. Color can be used as a quick reference for the different strategic options.

		1st end	Early 2nd/3rd end	Middle 4th/5th end	Late 6th end	7th end	8th end	Extra end
With last rock	Up by 2	X						
	Up by 1	X						
	Tied							
	Down by 1	X						
	Down by 2	X						
Without last rock	Up by 2	X						
	Up by 1	X						
	Tied							
	Down by 1	X						
	Down by 2	X						

Key: ▮ Defense   ▯ Balanced   ▯ Offense

Figure 8.10 Sample game plan.

In this case, the team has mapped out their preferences for various end, last-rock, and scoring possibilities and created a quick reference chart. Those strategic factors are not the only considerations, however. Tactical elements such as the ability of your team and your opponents, the ice conditions, whether the FGZ rule applies, and which player is throwing also need to be taken into account.

Shot calls that are simply beyond the ability of your team to throw are never good options. As players progress, they will discover the areas and shots they need to specifically improve to expand their toolbox. Your opponents' ability is a factor as well because every shot you complete sets the table for the opposition, and as your proficiency in calling a game advances, you will find that success often depends on what you leave your opponents rather than what you have done yourself. If you can put your opponents into a situation in which they are unable to make a shot easily, then you have gained an advantage over them.

MISSTEP

You call shots that your team can't make consistently.

CORRECTION

Keep a log or list of shots you and your team attempt that you do not make consistently, and add them to your regular practice. Also keep a mental list of shots you would like to be able to play but can't yet because of your skill development. Also add those shots to your training.

The ice conditions factor into your call with respect to both weight and the amount of curl on the sheet. Very straight ice can make it difficult to curl rocks around guards, for instance. In that case, it may not be easy or even possible to call a draw shot in a certain area, and so a different option would need to be explored.

The FGZ rule limits your shot selection in the early stages of an end. If the opponents place a guard, you may not be able to remove it per the rules, and so again, a different option needs to be found.

Which player is throwing is an important factor. You need to consider the player's ability and also where you are in an end. Given the exact same situational setup, it is unlikely that you would call the same shot for a second as you would for the skip. The more rocks there are to be played by both teams, the more foresight you need to employ during your shot selection. As the end nears completion, it may become time to play a risky shot, for example, something you wouldn't have done earlier with so many more stones left to come.

MISSTEP

You need to call a shot that is not your preference because a particular player on your team cannot throw the preferred shot.

CORRECTION

Make sure all players on the team gain proficiency in the shots their position demands through dedicated practice. Have your lead practice draws and guards. Seconds practice hits. Vices practice everything, and skips focus on draws. Eventually move beyond this and have all players gain proficiency in all shot making.

CALLING A SHOT

What has been described so far is the background needed in order to make specific shot calls. If you have a thorough understanding of the background, applying it becomes relatively simple. That does not suggest that choosing every shot will be simple, only that the thinking process behind the shot selection can now be simplified.

A simple process for calling a shot looks like this:

1. Prepare. Be aware of your team's preferences and abilities. Have a plan for the end based on the answers to the three big questions.

2. Analyze the options based on the current game situation. Which options fit your plan, style, and preferences? Who is throwing? How many stones are left to play? Which options can actually be made? Consider ice conditions, team ability, and whether the FGZ rule applies or has an impact. If you make the shot you want, what do you leave your opponent? Is that a situation you want? What are the risks involved with missing the shot you are looking at?

3. Choose the option you are most comfortable with, and call the shot with confidence.

It may seem like a simple process, but situations become complicated very quickly in a curling game, and you have a limited amount of time to make decisions. Having a process and the background to make decisions quickly is essential.

MISSTEP

You overestimate the ability of your team to make complicated shots and therefore call shots that have a lower likelihood of being made. This is common for new skips.

CORRECTION

Add a "gut check" to your shot-calling routine. Quickly analyze whether there is a simpler way to accomplish what you are attempting with your shot call and if your player can make the shot.

MISSTEP

You tend to neglect the risk versus reward analysis of a shot call. This is usually due to inexperience and an urgency to take care of the immediate situation without considering how the play will follow after the current shot.

CORRECTION

Watch games and try to anticipate a few shots ahead. Map out how you think the play will develop, and then carry that experience to your team. Alternatively, practice by playing the dice game as described next.

Strategy Drill 3   Dice Game

The dice game requires a portable strategy board of some sort that allows you to map out how a curling end might develop. This can be an electronic board or a magnetic board or even a handmade paper set of rings with coins. Any representation of the playing area will suffice. It also requires a six-sided die.

The game simulates a real curling end. Two players can play against each other, or team against team can work as well. Last-rock advantage is determined by any method the teams agree on. The team with the first shot must declare their intended shot. The die is tossed, and depending on the result, the shot is placed. Here is a possible set of results:

6: perfect shot as initially called

4 or 5: good shot, to the advantage of the throwing team but not perfect; throwing team gets to decide final result

2 or 3: slightly missed shot; the nonthrowing team gets to decide final result

1: complete miss; nonthrowing team gets to decide final result

The results you choose for the roll of the die can be changed if you want to skew it to a team with more or less skill. For example. if you want to skew the game towards a team with less skill, then the following rolls could yield the following results:

6: perfect shot as called

5: slightly missed shot with some advantage for the throwing team; throwing team gets to decide final result

4-3: missed shot; nonthrowing team gets some minor advantage as a result and nonthrowing team determines final result

2-1: complete miss; nonthrowing team gets a major advantage as a result of the shot

Once the first shot is "thrown," play proceeds as it would if you were on the ice. Because this is an exercise in strategy simulation, there should be lots of discussion about how the game will play out. This is a good way to gain some off-ice experience in decision making.

Success Check

- If playing with a team, collaborate with teammates on decisions. If playing one on one, think through each decision carefully before throwing the die.
- Be sure to follow the rules of curling.

Score Your Success

Earn 5 points for completing the game.

Your score ___

COMMON TACTICS

Although it is impossible to list every scenario, it is useful to examine the first few shots of a given end to help solidify your understanding of how to apply some of the strategies. Shots are thrown with the intention of gaining control over a piece of the playing area. The most valuable scoring area in the rings is a 4-foot (1.2 m) wide area that extends from in front of the tee line to the top of the house. This area is important for two reasons. First, from side to side in the rings, it is closest to the center. Just as important, however, when rocks are in front of the tee line, other stones coming to rest in front of them do not out-count them. Rocks in this prime piece of real estate can always be made better up until the point at which they are sitting on the center of the button, also known as the pin. This area is the most fought over piece of ice during a curling game.

Without Last Rock

Teams without last rock will throw the first rock of the end. This is the chance to exert control over this prime area. If a team without last rock wants to generate points, typically they will throw the first rock of the end as a center guard. The intention is to provide cover for a rock they will put into that 4-foot area later on and hopefully keep there as a scoring point. That guard, being one of the first four rocks of the end, cannot be removed because it is protected by the FGZ rule. The desired depth of that guard, or how close it is to the rings, will depend on ice conditions and what purpose the team wants it to serve. They may want to put up a subsequent center guard, which would lead them to throw the first one fairly close to the rings. It would be much easier to throw a second center guard in front of a previous stone rather than having to come around it, or they may want to use it as it is and draw a stone around it into the rings, leading them to throw it far enough in front of the rings so that a draw can be curled around it. If this is their intention, the guard should not be too far out because the long guard allows the opposition to follow the draw down with more weight and move the drawn stone out of play.

If a team without last rock wants to play defense, they will not put up a guard. Remember, defense is about keeping as few rocks in play as possible. One defensive option is to throw the first rock of the end through the rings, a strategy that can be particularly effective late in the game. The other defensive option for a first shot is to draw it into the middle of the house in front of the tee line. That shot is not protected by the FGZ rule and may be removed by the opposition. This is, in fact, what you hope your opponent will do if you are throwing a stone into that area as a first shot.

Those three shots (center guard, center draw, or throw-through) are pretty much the only shots called as an opening shot in an end. Occasionally a team will attempt to try to open an end by throwing something off the center; however, this is extremely uncommon and is usually the result of poor ice conditions and a desperate attempt to exploit them.

With Last Rock

Teams with last rock throw the second shot of an end and already face a large number of possible scenarios. If a team with last rock wants to play offensively, there are a couple of shots available. They may choose to throw a corner guard. This guard would be protected by the FGZ rule. It will give them some cover they may use later to secure a stone in a potential scoring position.

The other options depend on where their opponents have thrown. If a center guard is in play, then they may choose to draw around the center guard immediately. This will tend to concentrate play in that prime scoring area, however, and can make it difficult for teams with last rock to score more than 1 point.

If a team with last rock wants to play defensively, there are also a couple of options. First, they could choose to draw a stone into the rings in the wings (side of the rings) such that it is open and available to hit. The intention of this shot is to try to entice the opponent to hit it and therefore keep the playing area relatively clear.

The other defensive options depend on the situation. If a center guard is in place, the draw to the side of the house is available. The other option is to try to tick the center guard off that center position to open up the playing area. The center guard cannot be removed, but moving it such that there is no longer cover in front of the center area is the next best thing. If the opponents' rock is in the rings, simply removing it is the appropriate defensive option.

These brief examples assume that teams make the shots they attempt. In reality, and particularly early on in your curling efforts, these shots will not be made as perfectly as you might hope. That introduces a whole new set of considerations that cannot be planned for. Again, having a process and a plan will help you think through those situations.

Situations get exponentially more complicated as more rocks come into play. Certainly some ends are played cleanly by both teams—rocks are put into play and then a series of takeouts follow—but the entire game is unlikely to be played that way. It is much more common that the occasional end will be played clean, but most ends will see a variety of rock positions.

SUCCESS SUMMARY

Curling is deceptively elaborate. At first sight it looks very much like shuffleboard on ice, with stones simply sliding down to the other end; perhaps the earliest curling games were even like that. One can only imagine the consternation experienced by the first curling team that had a guard placed against them. Soon it must have followed that the opponents figured out how to draw in behind that cursed guard themselves, and from that point, it was game on.

Rocks do not have the variety of movements that chess pieces do, but they can move in more complex ways than shuffleboard discs, and that allows for more complex strategies. For many players, the cerebral challenge of the game is as alluring as the physical demands, and the combination of the two skill sets makes curling both a mental and physical workout.

Strategy in curling is not only for experienced players. Any game will quickly become boring if players do not understand why they are doing what they are doing. Every player on a team should understand what the shot calls are and what they are intended to accomplish. It keeps players engaged and better commits you to the success of the shot if you understand the purpose of it. The skills of strategy and shot calling in curling have a practically unlimited learning gradient that players can follow if they so desire. These skills fit hand in glove with physical prowess as well. As you gain more skill in throwing shots, your strategic views also expand because you gain more tools to play with.

For new players, understanding the basics of strategy is certainly enough to get you started and keep you engaged. New players will quickly experience situations that will confound them but will also help expand their strategic knowledge. If you absorb the background of what strategies are available and learn how they are put into practice, you will have a basis for applying the shot-calling process described. As a new player, you are not likely to start off calling shots as a skip, but knowing what is going on and applying some foresight makes the game infinitely more interesting at any position.

Each drill has been assigned a point value so you can evaluate your knowledge of curling strategy.

Strategy Drills

1.	Identify the Strategy	___ out of 10
2.	Pick a Strategy	___ out of 10
3.	Die Game	___ out of 5
	Your total	**___ out of 25**

A score of 15 or more indicates that you have a very good understanding of basic strategy. A score of 10 to 14 indicates you have a basic understanding of the principles, and a score of less than 10 indicates you need to review the material.

Mental Preparation and Goal Setting

As your individual curling skills improve, the game will present more challenges. Being a good thrower is not enough to be successful in the game, but it certainly is a good start. Your delivery and brushing technique should be the focus of your early curling efforts, but as your skill in these areas progresses, you will want to learn more about the game and expand your overall value as a player and teammate.

This step introduces you to a variety of topics that will crop up as you begin your journey in curling. It provides information and experience that will help you be a better teammate on your curling team.

MENTAL PREPARATION

Despite being a team game, curling can be very solitary. There is no getting around the fact that you and you alone will deliver two stones every end. Certainly you will have the support and direction of your teammates on all those shots, but recognizing that support isn't always simple, and you may feel considerable pressure when you settle in to throw your shots. The responsibility of those shots can weigh heavily on players during their deliveries, leading them to become distracted and concerned with issues that do not contribute to the success of the shot. There is a mental side of the game at all levels in curling, and so it is worth spending some time addressing how to handle those particular challenges. At the game's highest levels, teams spend significant amounts of time improving their mental game, to the extent of getting professional direction. Most top-level teams employ a mental coach to some degree, and although you may not be aiming for that level of competition, the pressures you face will be challenging enough to warrant some attention.

Mental preparation is an extensive area of study, and this is not meant to cover the myriad topics within it. In The Sport of Curling, we discuss what a physical warm-up should consist of. That process prepares your body for the activity you are about to perform by warming up your muscles. Your warm-up routine is also a good time to get your thoughts in order. Before a game at any level, excitement or anxiety can hamper your efforts once you step on the ice. Working to develop your mind-set before the game is an excellent way to begin your mental preparation.

Mentally preparing for a game is a little different from the physical preparation because each player needs something different to get into an ideal performance state. Some people will need something to pick up their energy, while others will need something to calm them. Some people will need some solitude to think through what they are about to do, and others require some social interaction. Before working out your pregame mental routine, you need to first understand yourself and your own needs. Most of the time this is going to come from experience. Look back at other performances in other sports or activities, and think about what you did before your most successful ones. Were you jazzed up? Were you mellow and relaxed? Typically, finding your ideal performance state will take a little bit of trial and error and quite a lot of private introspection.

Once you've discovered where you need to steer your personal excitement level, you can start to develop an appropriate pregame routine that will get you there. There are many effective methods for both energizing yourself and calming yourself before a game. Music can be a very powerful way to adjust your mood and excitement level. Choose music that you personally enjoy listening to but that also helps guide your mood in the right direction. If you prefer not to listen to music before games, you can certainly find other appropriate activities to adjust your mood. The physical warm-up can be a good way to energize yourself, particularly if you perform it with your team. If, however, you need some calming after the physical warm-up, you may choose to take a few minutes to retire to the change room and review some technical points of the delivery as a way of calming down and centering your mind. Deep breathing exercises are an excellent method of relaxing and bringing down your excitement level if required.

Another important mental skill for beginners to develop is your ability to focus and to recognize what you should be focusing on. Focus in curling primarily consists of two parts: ignoring distractions and concentrating on the things you personally control. As you progress in the game, you will want to expand your efforts in mental preparation, but for now it is enough to examine your delivery and what you should be thinking when you are about to throw a rock.

After all you have learned about the curling delivery, it will sound odd to hear that you really don't have control over the outcome of your shot. There are simply too many factors that can affect the stone as it travels down the ice. The ice conditions, the stone itself, your brushers, and your skip, just to name a few, all have an effect on the shot after you release it, and so the final outcome is literally out of your hands. The impact you have on the shot is based on your interaction with the stone, and so that is where your mind should be directed. Concentrate on the physical process of your delivery because that is the only thing you actually have control over.

Developing a routine that you follow for each shot is one way to maintain the correct focus. If you perform the same actions every time you get into the hack to throw, it can help you be more consistent during the actual delivery. It also gives you a familiar checklist you can review, and that review will help focus your mind on the specific thoughts you should be concerned with. As you practice, you may discover that parts of your delivery need more work than others, and so part of your shot routine may include a reminder of how you want to perform that particular action. For example, once you are settled into the hack, you may want to repeat a simple phrase such as "wrist high" when you apply your grip to remind you how that grip should feel. Another example might be something related to the line if that is an area on which you want to concentrate. Using a simple phrase such as "straight up the line" can help direct your thoughts toward positive actions.

We are always talking to ourselves within our own minds, and so keeping our self-messages positive is a powerful way to keep our outlook and mood positive. Your self-messages in your preshot routine should never be negative and should always focus on things within your control. At some point you will find yourself saying negative things to yourself or at least things that do not contribute to the action you are about to perform. "I better not mess up like last time" is a negative thought that focuses on things outside your control. Even something like "if I make this shot we'll be in really good shape" is not actually positive. With that particular phrase, you are focused on the outcome of the shot rather than on the process that you control. When you identify these negative thoughts creeping into your self-talk, you need to first recognize that they do nothing to help you perform. Second, you need to replace that line of thought with something that is positive and within your control. Having a short script or list of acceptable phrases you have identified before your games can help you break out of this negative line of thinking. Once again, something like "feet parallel in the setup" or "back straight and shoulders square" are good positive reinforcements of things you can control.

Of course, you do not have to deal with these issues all by yourself. Teams should discuss how to encourage each other during play by talking about what helps each person. Some people like to hear encouragement, while others need something concrete to help them focus. Some players want some quiet time to prepare. It should be the goal of every team to learn what each of their teammates needs before her shot.

Build a preshot routine—a relatively short mental checklist of actions you perform each and every shot—and make sure the elements of that routine are rooted in the performance factors you have learned so far. The routine should not be complicated and should not include anything that does not contribute to the shot. It will be unique to you and should be somewhat fluid. Certainly the point of a routine is to bring some feeling of familiarization to your mind before a shot, but if you identify a step that isn't helping, get rid of it! Similarly, if you think your preshot routine is missing a critical item, then add it. The routine is yours to develop and revise. This one simple action will help you start each and every shot on a positive mental note, and it will help you focus on the things within your control.

An example of a preshot routine follows:

1. Set gripper foot in hack, pointing to the target
2. Double-check grip on your brush
3. Check that your feet are positioned with slider-foot heel even with gripper toe
4. Pause and take a deep breath before starting your delivery

Again, this list will be completely different for every player and should be built to suit individual needs. Take some time to identify the factors you personally need to reinforce.

MISSTEP

You repeatedly get frustrated with results in a game.

CORRECTION

Examine what you are thinking during your moments of frustration. Are they factors within your control? If so, then focus on the physical changes you can make that will have an effect on the outcomes. If not, reset your focus on things you can control.

MISSTEP

You repeat delivery mistakes in your setup.

CORRECTION

Review your preshot routine, and ensure there is a step that addresses the error in a way you can control it.

GOAL SETTING

Players who want to improve their skills and progress in the game of curling make considerable use of goal setting. Goal setting also aids in mental preparation because it focuses your efforts in practice and during competition on things that are important to you personally. Since you have made the decision to try the sport and have made some commitment to improving your skills, your efforts should have some direction, and setting appropriate goals is a positive first step. In fact, as you have seen in the strategy section, you need to set goals during a game as well. Incorporating goal setting into your regular routine is a good way to practice that particular skill set.

Goals are meant to motivate you and keep you involved by challenging you as well as by setting a target for you to hit. One of the more tried and true models for setting goals is the SMART model first proposed by George T. Doran in the November 1981 issue of *Management Review*. It is commonly used by curlers and curling teams to set both individual goals and team goals.

SMART is an acronym that represents the elements that should be contained in every goal.

Specific. Goals should define what you are trying to achieve. "Getting better" is vague and too difficult to define, but "sliding without my slider foot wobbling" is much more specific.

Measurable. How can you know if you are improving if you do not measure your performance? The drills in this book are scored for that very purpose. Assigning a measurement to goals can be challenging, but it is essential if you are to track your progress.

Achievable. The goals you set must be achievable but not easy. The goal of making it to the next Olympics is not achievable if you are just starting out. Playing in two bonspiels in the upcoming season is achievable. Goals are meant to be challenging. If you are constantly achieving every goal you set, perhaps you need to aim higher. On the other hand, never achieving a goal becomes demoralizing. A decent benchmark is a 75 percent achievement rate. Always push yourself to do better.

Relevant. The goals you set must relate to what you are trying to accomplish. Setting a goal as a skip, for instance, of "being able to brush 8 straight rocks and being able to recover my heart rate to its normal resting rate within 20 seconds" is a great fitness goal but it's not really where a skip should be putting his training efforts.

Time based. If a goal does not have a time associated with it, then it will be allowed to slip. "Winning four games" is a pretty likely occurrence if you do not put a time boundary on it. "Winning four games this season" is much better.

Beginners starting out should set some personal goals for their own development. Working with a coach or mentor can help with this process immensely. Another important component of goal setting is tracking. Ideally, you will have a mix of short- and long-term goals, all leading to higher challenges. But if you simply write them out and put them into a drawer, then goals do not serve the purpose they are intended to. Keep them visible, and refer to them often.

Finally, when you do achieve a goal, celebrate it. This whole exercise is meant to inspire and motivate you, and curling is an ideal sport for celebration with its history of social interaction. You won't have much difficulty finding someone to help you celebrate a curling achievement. You should look forward to achieving the goals you set for yourself, and celebrating them is an ideal way to keep yourself motivated.

MISSTEP
You set goals that aren't SMART.

CORRECTION
Review each goal against the SMART criteria, and identify the necessary factors.

MISSTEP
You don't set enough goals.

CORRECTION
Set goals that cover all the areas where you want to see improvement or achieve something. You should not have so many goals that you can't keep track of them all, but you should set goals around all the areas that are important to you.

SUCCESS SUMMARY

You must have some motivation already if you are willing to try to learn the game of curling. Something has made you decide there are rewards to be had through your involvement in this sport. One major source of frustration for new curlers is the feeling that they are not progressing by improving skills or learning more about the game. The mental side of curling can be an unrecognized source of frustration as well. By spending some of your efforts on mentally preparing yourself to play, you give yourself a much better chance of enjoying your experience and thus sticking with the game long enough to see your physical skills improve. Appropriate goal setting will keep your motivations fresh in the game and help you constantly find new challenges and rewards that will make your curling experience a great one.

Mixed Doubles

Mixed doubles curling is a relatively new discipline of the game that has started to gain popularity around the world. The first mixed doubles world championship was held in 2008, and in June of 2015 the International Olympic Committee announced that mixed doubles curling would be included in the 2018 Winter Games to be held in Pyeongchang, South Korea. This is a phenomenal rise in profile for a discipline of curling that did not exist much in any official form before 2005. The rapid expansion and acceptance of mixed doubles events are great endorsements for the sport as a whole and provide an avenue to a different type of competition while maintaining much of the traditional game.

RULES AND HOW TO PLAY

A mixed doubles curling team consists of a pair of players, one male and the other female. Standard curling sheets are used, and normal delivery rules apply. Typically games are eight ends in length. Thankfully, the skills you have learned up to this point still apply in the game of mixed doubles. The real changes are in how the game proceeds.

Each team throws five rocks rather than eight. One player throws the first and fifth stones, and the other player throws the second, third, and fourth stones. Teams may choose to change which of the pair throws the first and fifth stones from end to end. This is one major difference from the four-person game, where players cannot rotate positions within a game.

Each team has one additional stone placed within the playing area at one of two specific spots on the sheet. To be clear, each team gets six stones that can potentially be in play. They throw only five of those stones, since both teams have one stone in play before the end begins.

The first placement option is behind the tee line at the center line, touching the 4-foot circle as shown in figure 10.1. The second option is a center guard, the depth of which is predetermined before the game and depends on the amount of curl on the sheet. If conditions allow for more curl, the guard placement is closer to the rings. Standard placement is about halfway between the rings and the hog line. Figure 10.1 shows the three possible placements for the yellow stone, only one of which will be used throughout the game.

In the traditional team game, the team with the hammer throws the second stone of the end. In mixed doubles, however, the team with the hammer gets to choose rock placement, which in turn determines who throws last rock. The team whose rock is placed out front of the house must throw the first rock of the end. The result of this rule is that the team with the hammer may choose to throw the first rock of the next end if they choose to position their stone out front of the rings to start the end.

The next major difference between the mixed doubles game and the traditional team game is with respect to the free guard zone rule. Recall that in the traditional game, your team is not allowed to remove an opposing rock positioned within the free guard zone (FGZ) until the fifth shot of the end. Stones within the rings are allowed to be removed under this rule, and you can remove your own stones if you so desire even if they are in the free guard zone. The modified FGZ rule in mixed doubles states that no rocks, even the ones initially placed to start the end, may be removed before the fourth delivered rock of the end. This means rocks in the rings and guards are all protected until that shot. Also, it means you cannot remove your own guards or stones in the rings. If a violation of this rule occurs, the stones are repositioned at the discretion of the nonoffending team to where they were before the shot, and the shot is considered spent. To help clarify how this works, if team A throws first in the end, that shot cannot be a takeout of any stone. Team B's first shot, the second shot of the end, also cannot be a takeout. Team A's second shot, the third of the end, cannot be a takeout, but team B's second shot, being the fourth shot of the end, may be a takeout. Every shot from there on during the end may be a takeout if desired.

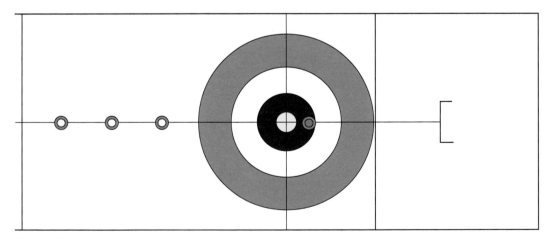

Figure 10.1   Initial setup.

Scoring in mixed doubles is the same as it is in the traditional team game, and the two initial stones are eligible to be counted if they are moved into a scoring position. Hammer determination during game play is the same as for the four-person game; however, *hammer* has a slightly different meaning in that the team that scored gets a choice of rock placement and accompanying throwing order rather than automatic last-rock advantage. One other slight change to the scoring rules is that if an end is blanked (i.e., no team scores), then the hammer, or decision on initial rock placement, changes between teams. In the traditional game, blanking an end is a tactic that can be used to maintain last-rock advantage into a subsequent end. In mixed doubles, a blank means losing the advantage of hammer.

DELIVERING AND BRUSHING

Delivering stones in mixed doubles is the same as it is in the traditional game. The techniques and skills you have worked on up to this point are all applied exactly the same. The same rules also apply with respect to the delivery. Stones must be released before the hog line, and once a stone has crossed the near tee line in a delivery, it is considered played. Of course, because the game is played on the same ice with the same stones as the traditional game, all the implications of curl and ice speed remain the same in mixed doubles.

One major difference regarding the delivery is the intended target placement. The rocks will still curl as usual, but in the traditional team game the skip holds the brush for the thrower as a target. That target is placed with an educated estimate of how much curl the shot will have. Mixed doubles does not require that one of the pair of players stay in the house for the purpose of providing a target for the thrower. The nonthrowing partner may be positioned anywhere, including at the throwing end to help the thrower decide on the shot and target while being in place to brush the upcoming shot. This means there may be no target at the far end for the thrower. Mixed doubles teams therefore need to learn to read ice and adjust delivery paths from the throwing end while using some existing feature at the far end as a delivery target.

POWER PLAY

The power play is an option teams may use once per game when they have the hammer. The power play is a different arrangement of the initial two stones (figure 10.2). Instead of one rock behind the tee line on the button, the stone in the rings is placed such that the back edge touches the tee line, with half the stone in the 12-foot ring and half in the 8-foot ring. This is shown as the red rock in figure 10.2. The opponents' stone is placed as a perfect guard on this rock in the rings as shown by the yellow rock in figure 10.2. This arrangement may be set up on either side of the sheet as chosen by the team exercising the power play. The team with the hammer who is exercising the power play will then have last-rock advantage in the end, and the other team will throw the first stone of the end.

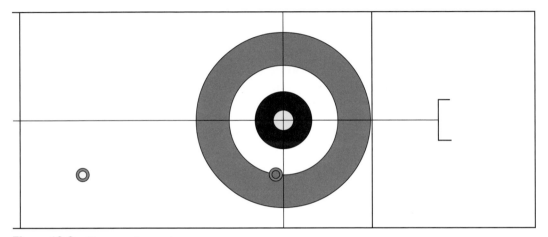

Figure 10.2 Power play setup.

STRATEGY

The game of mixed doubles takes the traditional game and skews it toward an aggressive style of play. Recall from what you learned in step 8, Basic Strategy, that when playing an aggressive or offensive style, the goal is to get rocks into play. Mixed doubles rules lead to both teams playing an aggressive style. Other than the modified free guard zone rule, there are no restrictions on what shots you are allowed to play, so you are not specifically prevented from playing a defensive game if you so wish, but with the placement of two stones on the ice before the start of play, simply trying to remove rocks to reduce the chance of scoring becomes much more difficult.

Any kind of defense you mount is more likely to be an attempt to reposition rocks in play to reduce the scoring area for your opponents. Certainly you can play takeouts, but in mixed doubles a lot of rocks are in play very quickly, and removing all the stones causing your team trouble can be a nearly impossible task.

The game requires all the same skills but does skew toward finesse shots. Successful players need to have a very good feel for draw weight and good knowledge of angles. Draw weight, already extremely important in the traditional game, becomes even more essential because you have only one brusher to aid your rock on any given shot. Knowledge of angles is critical because of the number of rocks in play. In mixed doubles, you will face complicated situations more often and will need to use the rocks in play to reposition your stones.

The following drills focus on weight control and on delicate movement of stones within the playing area. These typical skills required in the mixed doubles game do not differ from what is required in the traditional game. Before attempting these drills, you should review steps 2, 3, and 4 so you are comfortable with adjusting weight and line accurately.

MISSTEP

Your shots are consistently heavy.

CORRECTION

Discuss the weight with your partner, and adjust so that your partner needs to brush the stone to get it into position.

MISSTEP

Your shots have the correct weight but do not stop on the target because the line is not correct.

CORRECTION

Discuss with your partner what line you are throwing your rocks down, and adjust it either in or out depending on how you are missing the shots.

MISSTEP

You are not throwing enough weight to promote the target rock into the rings.

CORRECTION

Make a significant weight adjustment. Remember, particularly on the first shots, that each rock in the line will bleed off some energy so that the amount of energy the final rock in the line has will be significantly reduced from what you initially threw.

Mixed Doubles Drill 1   Grab the Button

Developing draw weight is critical for success in mixed doubles. This drill helps you improve your weight-control skills. The drill is performed with a partner who will brush your shots. Throw eight shots, with the goal of having your stone come to rest on the button at the far end. Each shot must alternate handles (turns) from the previous; if your first shot has a clockwise rotation, the next shot must have a counterclockwise rotation. After each shot comes to rest, remove the stone just thrown. Each shot should be thrown to an empty playing area. Scores for each shot depends on what ring your rock stops on.

TO INCREASE DIFFICULTY

- Do not count any points unless your rock stops in the 4-foot ring or button. Alternatively, place a center guard in play as would be seen on the first rock of a normal mixed doubles game. Contact with the guard automatically gives you 0 points on that shot.

TO DECREASE DIFFICULTY

- Adjust the scoring so that 5 points are awarded for stopping on the 4-foot ring. Deduct 1 point for landing on each subsequent ring.

Success Check

- Do not overthrow your rocks. That is, throw less weight rather than more so your partner has the opportunity to help make the shot.
- Remember, there will be no skip to choose the correct target at the far end, so you need to gauge this yourself with the help of your partner.

Score Your Success

Earn points depending on where your shot stops.

5 points: button

4 points: 4-foot ring

3 points: 8-foot ring

2 points: 12-foot ring

1 point: outside the rings but in play

Your score ___

Mixed Doubles Drill 2   Arrowhead

Set up one set of stones in front of the far set of rings as shown in figure 10.3. The stones are lined up in an arrowhead configuration in front of the rings. Have a partner with you to brush your shots. Throw seven shots with the goal of promoting all seven yellow stones into the rings. After each shot, remove the shooter, but do not reposition the yellow stones that remain outside the rings. Rocks that are promoted into the rings are scored depending on where they end up and then immediately removed. Any disturbance of the rocks out front is left as is, and you will have to figure out how to use the resulting angles to promote stones into the rings. The purpose of the drill is to develop your skill with tapping stones at specific angles to put them into position. This is a common skill required in mixed doubles.

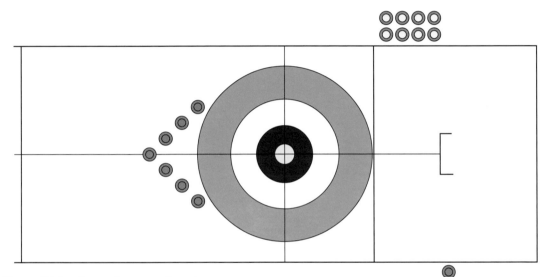

Figure 10.3   Setup for arrowhead.

 TO INCREASE DIFFICULTY

- Position the stones farther from the rings. The farther they are from the house the more precise the contact angles will need to be.

 TO DECREASE DIFFICULTY

- Use five stones at the top of the house in the initial setup rather than seven.

Success Check

- Gauge the target so that your thrown stone makes contact in the center of the lead stationary stone.
- Gauge the weight needed to promote each stone into the rings but no farther.
- Adjust your weight to compensate for the various distances due to the angles of the stones.

Score Your Success

Points are counted for where the promoted rocks stop in the rings. Points are assigned as follows:

5 points: button

4 points: 4-foot ring

3 points: 8-foot ring

2 points: 12-foot ring

Your score ___

CHOOSING A TEAMMATE

A mixed doubles team consists of only two players, and so forming a team is that much simpler. At the beginner level, this factor contributes to its popularity since managing and scheduling two people is much easier than it is for four people. Just as with the traditional game, there needs to be some connection between partners in mixed doubles. It could be argued that this connection must be even closer than in a four-person team because of the constant interaction between partners on every facet of game play. Often couples will play as a team since there is already some existing connection between them. At higher levels, people will consider performance factors when choosing their teammate rather than simply playing with a friend.

Team dynamics still factor heavily into your choice for a teammate. If there is little room to hide issues on a four-person team, there is obviously less room to hide them on a two-person team. Partners must have a similar attitude toward the game and similar aspirations, just as in the four-person game. They should share similar goals and motivations and have a similar disposition in how they prefer to approach strategy. This is actually less of a factor than with the four-person version because mixed doubles is so heavily skewed toward an aggressive, offense-first style of game. Highly defensive-minded players will have to find their inner aggressor to adapt to mixed doubles.

This doesn't mean that the skills required to play a defensive game aren't important or that defensive players can't be successful. Recall that defensive play means removing stones and decreasing the opportunity to score. Often this is accomplished with takeout-style shots. Because of the complicated angles that result in mixed doubles play, the ability to hit and roll accurately is an important skill. Defensive players count these hit and roll shots as their best.

When looking for a mixed doubles partner, you need to be honest about your abilities and weaknesses. Ideally, your partner should complement your abilities. If you have particular weaknesses, then your ideal teammate will have those skills as strengths. Because mixed doubles allows you to switch the throwing order from end to end, you have some ability to adjust when particular skills are needed during the game.

At its core, the game of mixed doubles is still curling, however, so the skill sets developed to play the traditional team game are all still required for this specific discipline. Brushing factors heavily into the mixed doubles game because all players must be ready to brush stones. The skills are the same, but in mixed doubles you are brushing alone, and so the judgment for weight rests on your shoulders. If anything, this means the skills you previously developed need to be even more finely tuned.

Since all players are expected to sweep, fitness is a priority for both players. In addition to brushing stones by yourself, the mixed doubles game moves faster than the team game, and so recovery and conditioning factor into this discipline very heavily.

Players should also look for partners who have a good knowledge of both strategy and how rocks move and react. Ends get complicated in this game, and there will be a lot of rocks in play. Partners need to be able to quickly think through the options and combinations in order to be successful. Also, you will be required to make shots that make use of other rocks in play. Knowing how the rocks will behave is an important factor in making run-back shots, angle raises, and hit and roll shots.

More than anything, however, when choosing a mixed doubles teammate, you should be looking for compatibility. Two good players don't necessarily make a good mixed doubles team if they don't see eye to eye.

SUCCESS SUMMARY

Mixed doubles is an aggressive and much faster-paced version of the traditional game. Both beginners and experienced players are embracing this version for a number of reasons. While adding a number of specific rules, mixed doubles is still true to the traditional game with respect to the overall goals of game play. You still need to fight to get your stones closest to the center of the rings in order to score. Fitness and brushing skills come into play significantly in mixed doubles as well because there is only one brusher. To make a significant impact, that brusher has to do the job that two people do in the traditional game. At the social and beginner levels, the game has many advantages over the traditional game. Couples can play in leagues without having to find and schedule another pair of players. The game is also much faster because you throw fewer rocks and because fewer players are involved. Compared with the traditional game, there is very little time spent waiting for your turn. The speed of the game is an attraction for couples who want some activity but don't want to dedicate two hours or more in an evening. A full mixed doubles game can take place in a little over one hour.

With its inclusion in the Olympic Games, mixed doubles has entrenched itself into the curling world. Although still in its infancy, its rapid expansion speaks volumes about its longevity.

Each drill has been assigned a point value so you can evaluate your progress in some skills needed to be successful in the mixed doubles game.

Mixed Doubles Drills

1. Grab the Button   ___ out of 40

2. Arrowhead   ___ out of 35

    Total   **___ out of 75**

A total combined score of 59 or more indicates that you have successfully developed significant throwing skills required in mixed doubles. A score between 48 and 58 indicates you have gained some proficiency, and a score below 48 indicates you should review the skills and continue to practice them.

Glossary

advanced closed stance—A brushing technique where the player's hips are closed to the direction of travel. The advanced stance has components that go beyond the standard closed stance.

back end—The skip and the vice as a pair are referred to as back-end players.

back up – A description of the curl of a stone that is opposite from what is expected. See "fall".

blank end—An end in curling where neither team scores any points. This can be used deliberately by teams to maintain last-rock advantage into the subsequent end.

bonspiel—A curling tournament.

break point—The point in a shot at which the rock begins to curl.

brick – Rocks have a variety of colloquial terms applied to them. Sometimes a rock will be referred to as a brick. A common use of this is to refer to the last shot of the end as "throwing the last brick".

brush—A piece of curling equipment consisting of a brushing device at the end of a long shaft. The brush is used for brushing the ice and to help stabilize a player during delivery.

brushing—The act of cleaning the path in front of the stone as it travels down the sheet during a shot. Brushing also polishes the ice surface to help keep the stone moving and reduces the amount of curl.

bury—Refers to placing a shot behind one or more stones already in play. The more covered the shot is, the better it is buried.

button—The centermost circle in the rings.

center guards—Rocks positioned toward the middle of the sheet to keep opponents from accessing a specific area.

clean—There are two meanings for *clean*. It can refer to lightly brushing the path of a stone as it travels, thus keeping the path clean. It can also refer to a style of play whereby few stones are in play, thus keeping the playing area clean.

closed stance—A brushing technique where the player's hips are closed to the direction of travel.

corn broom—A straw broom that can be used to sweep in front of curling stones. Corn brooms are practically never used anymore and have been replaced by other devices.

corner guards—Rocks positioned toward the edges of the sheet to keep opponents from accessing a specific area.

curl—The amount of curve in the path of a stone as it travels down the sheet.

curling sheet—The area of ice where a curling game is played. Often, this is simply referred to as a sheet.

curling stone—A piece of granite that is thrown down the curling sheet during a game. Curling stones are the objects used to play the game of curling.

directional brushing—A brushing technique that is different from the traditional method of brushing. It involves brushing a part of the path of the stone to make the stone change direction more drastically than would normally be experienced.

drag effect—This describes how two stationary stones that are touching will move when contacted by a moving stone. The effect is counter intuitive.

draw league—A curling league where players are assigned to teams for a specific period and then rotated to different teams. Typically there are a number of these draws throughout the season.

draw shot—A shot intended to stop within the playing area on its own without contacting other stones.

double or double takeout—A shot that is intended to remove two stones from play with one shot.

dumping—When brushing, stopping the brushing stroke in the path of delivery thereby dropping or "dumping" debris in the path to potentially slow a rock that has too much weight.

end—A division of play in a curling game. Each game consists of a predetermined number of ends, similar to innings in baseball.

extra end—A tie-breaking end played after the scheduled end of a game in order to break a tie, often simply known as an extra. It is analogous to overtime.

fall—This describes the curl of a rock when it is opposite of what is expected. See "back up".

FGZ—Acronym for free guard zone. See free guard zone.

finish—The last bit of motion on a curling stone during a shot, often a pronounced movement as the rock loses the last of its momentum.

flat spots—Sections of the ice where the pebble has worn away and become ineffective; these spots may cause shots to travel severely off their intended path.

force—A scoring situation whereby the team without last rock forces the team with last rock to take a single point rather than two points. Often forcing the opposition to take a single point is the goal of the team without last-rock advantage.

freeze—A shot that is intended to stop immediately in front of and in contact with a stone already in play.

free guard zone—The area in front of the tee line but outside the rings. The free guard zone rule states that you may not remove an opponent's stone from the free guard zone until the fifth rock of the end.

front end—The second and lead as a pair are referred to as the front-end players.

fudging—When the pebble wears down a common path on a curling sheet, that path can get much slower relative to the rest of the sheet. That effect is sometimes called "fudging". Worn pebble is also referred to as "flat" ice.

gripper foot—The foot that has a material applied to the sole to improve traction on the ice during game play.

guard—A shot that is intended to protect a situation in play or to create a protected area. A stone in play that serves this function will be referred to as a guard regardless of how it was achieved as well.

hack—A rubber block at the end of each sheet of ice from which players propel themselves into their deliveries.

hammer—Last-rock advantage in an end.

handle—Often refers to the direction of rotation a curling stone has. Skips will call the handle as clockwise or counterclockwise. Also referred to as the turn.

heavy—An indication of speed or weight of a rock. Heavy means a faster speed.

hit—See takeout. A shot thrown with the intention of contacting a stone already in play.

hit and roll—A takeout shot where the shooter is intended to hit a stone at an angle and then roll to a specific area of the sheet.

hog line—A line on a curling sheet that defines how far stones must travel in order to remain in play. It also identifies the distance a player may hold on to a stone before releasing it.

hog to hog timing—A timing method that uses the time a rock takes to travel between the hog lines to help aid in ice reading.

house—Also known as the rings, a set of concentric rings at the end of each curling sheet that serve as the scoring area.

in and off—A hit and roll where the shooter gets in a specific position by hitting and coming off another stone in play.

interval timing—A method for gauging the speed of stones during a delivery.

in-turn—The rotation applied during a shot. An in-turn is clockwise rotation for a right-handed player and counterclockwise rotation for a left-handed player.

jam—A situation whereby a takeout shot is attempted and the stone to be removed contacts another stone in play and therefore does not leave the playing area. The shot is said to have "jammed" on the rock that was deeper in play.

lead—The player on a curling team who delivers the team's first two stones.

leg drive—The act of extending the gripper leg to push your body into the slide position.

line—The path a curling stone is taking. It may also refer to the initial target down which a player is attempting to deliver.

light—An indication of speed or weight of a shot. Light means a slower speed.

long guard—A guard far from the top of the rings. A long guard is usually closer to the hog line than the rings.

mate—See vice skip.

negative ice—When rocks curl in the opposite direction than expected they are said to fall. Negative ice refers to a piece of ice where rocks fall.

nipper—A blade mounted on a handle that is used to prepare ice.

nipping—The act of using a nipper to prepare the ice before the game by cutting the tops off the pebble.

normal weight—A standard speed that teams decide will be their default speed on takeout shots.

no-lift delivery—A curling delivery method whereby the player does not lift the stone off the ice at any point during the delivery.

nose hit—A takeout shot where the shooter is not intended to move after contact with the target stone.

open league—A curling league that allows any combination of men, women, or youth on a team rather than conventional team formations.

open stance—A brushing technique where the player's hips are open and square to the direction of travel.

out-turn—Refers to the rotation applied during a shot. An out-turn is counterclockwise rotation for a right-handed player and clockwise rotation for a left-handed player.

path of delivery—See line of delivery.

pebble—Small bumps of ice on the surface of the curling sheet, applied to the sheet on purpose to reduce friction.

peel—A shot that is intended to remove stones from play but also requires that the shooter roll out. *Peel* can also refer to a weight designation.

pick—A shot that has accumulated debris under it as it travels down the ice; usually this ruins the shot. A pick may also be caused by flat ice, again ruining the shot.

pin—The center of the button. There is a small indentation in the center of the button to allow a measuring device to be placed there if required. A rock on the pin cannot be out-counted by any other stone.

release point—The place where the player delivering the stone actually releases it.

rings—Also known as the house, a set of concentric rings at the end of each sheet that serve as the scoring area.

rocking—The act of dragging a set of rocks down a freshly pebbled sheet to help break in the surface before game play.

run back—A shot that is intended to promote a stone in play into another stone in play to remove the second, deeper stone.

second—The player on a curling team who throws the team's second pair of stones.

set or setting—Putting the stone off the line of delivery during the release.

sheet—See curling sheet.

shooter—The rock that was delivered rather than any of the other rocks that may be set in motion as a result of a shot.

short guard—A guard placed close to the rings. Usually a short guard is closer to the rings than the hog line. It may also refer to how far away the guard is from the stone it is protecting. A short guard is close to its protected stone.

shot rock—This refers to the first counting stone, the one that is in the rings and on the rings therefore eligible to count as a point. Shot rock does not become a scored point until the conclusion of an end but it is common to refer to the primary counter during the end as "shot rock".

skip—The player who directs the team on which shot to throw and who throws the last pair of stones for the team.

slide path—The path taken by the player as she delivers the rock; sometimes also refers to the path the stone takes after release.

slider foot—The foot that has material applied to the sole to reduce friction during game play. This is the foot that supports the player during the delivery.

soft weight—Another way to refer to light weight on a shot.

spinner—A shot with an extreme amount of rotation.

steal—When a team without last rock scores points.

straight ice—Ice conditions that do not permit much curl; this is a relative term and is used to compare conditions.

straw broom—See corn broom.

sweeping—See brushing.

synthetic—Another way to refer to fabric covered brushes.

takeout shot—A shot intended to remove stones from play.

tap back—A shot intended to push a stationary rock in play deeper into the playing area without removing it from play.

tee line—A line that bisects the rings across the width of the sheet. It is the point of no return for a curling shot—once a stone has crossed this line, it is in play.

thinking time—A method for timing a curling game whereby teams are allotted a certain amount of time per game to call all their shots.

third—See vice skip.

throw-through—A shot call where the rock is intended to be played through the house without stopping and without making contact with any rocks in play.

tick shot—A shot that is intended to contact a rock protected by the free guard zone rule and move it from its location without removing it from play.

top of the house—The area of the house (rings) that is closest to the hog line.

turn—See handle. This refers to the rotation that is applied to the stone during the delivery.

vice skip—Also known as the third or mate. The player who takes over for the skip when the skip delivers his stones. Also, the player who throws the third pair of stones for the team.

weight—The amount of force put on a stone during a delivery.

wings—The sides of the sheet or house. Throwing a shot to the wings means throwing it so that it ends up away from the center line.

Additional Resources

HISTORY OF CURLING

World Curling Federation: www.worldcurling.org/history-of-curling

RULES

World Curling Federation: www.worldcurling.org/
rules-and-regulations-downloads

CURLING FEDERATIONS

Canadian Curling Association: www.curling.ca

US Curling Association: www.teamusa.org/USA-Curling

Scottish Curling Association: www.royalcaledoniancurlingclub.org

World Curling Federation: www.worldcurling.org

Curling Federations around the world: www.worldcurling.org/
wcf-member-associations

CURLING CAMPS

www.wcf-camps-courses.com

www.hotshotscurling.com

trilliumcurlingcamp.com

amethystcurling.com

www.fourfootcurling.com

www.curlbc.ca/coursescamps/rockslide-camps/rockslide/

curling.savillecentre.ca/

www.turningpointcurling.com

OTHER

www.curlingzone.com

thecurlingnews.com

About the Author

Sean Turriff is a National Coaching Certification Program (NCCP) Competition Development certified coach as well as a coach evaluator and learning facilitator through the Ontario Curling Association and Canadian Curling Association. He is also the men's varsity curling coach at Humber College, Toronto, winners of the 2016 CCAA National Men's Curling Championship.

In 2015, Turriff had the distinction of being camp director for the Chinese National Junior Curling Camp in Shanghai on behalf of the World Curling Federation. Since 2011, Turriff has coached at the Trillium Junior Curling Camp in Ontario, working with the highest level of curling coaches in Canada. In addition, he coached the Brandon University (Brandon, Manitoba) women's team in the Canadian University Championships in 2007-08, and he was coach of the 2016 Nunavut junior men's team when they won their first game ever at a national competition at the Canadian Junior Curling Championships.

Off the sheet, Turriff has served as an on-air commentator for curling competitions broadcast on Rogers TV. Turriff's unique background in coaching at all levels of competition, coach training and evaluation, international coaching, and television commentary make him a highly respected expert and ambassador of the sport.

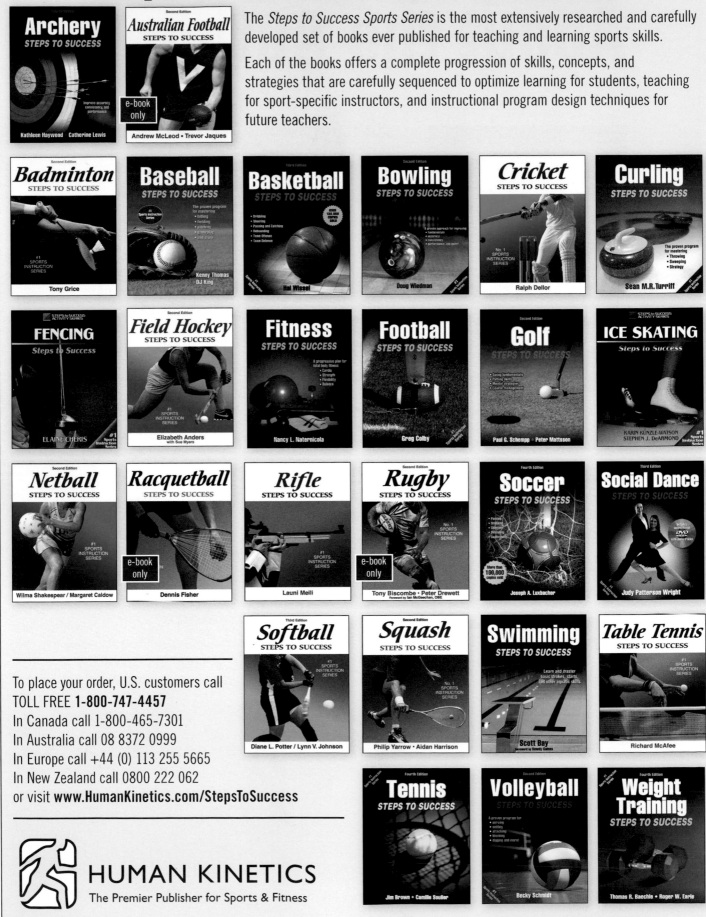
JAN 1 9 2017